Inspector Morse
Country

Inspector Morse Country

An Illustrated Guide to the World of Oxford's Famous Detective

CLIFF GOODWIN

headline

Also by Cliff Goodwin
Sid James: A Biography
Evil Spirits: The Life of Oliver Reed
When the Wind Changed: The Life and Death of Tony Hancock
To Be a Lady: The Story of Catherine Cookson
Richard Harris: Behaving Badly

First published in 2002
by HEADLINE BOOK PUBLISHING

10 9 8 7 6 5 4 3 2 1

Cataloguing in Publication Data is available from the British Library.

ISBN: 0 7553 1064 0

Printed and bound in Italy by Canale & C. Spa

Design by Ben Cracknell Studios

HEADLINE BOOK PUBLISHING
A division of Hodder Headline
338 Euston Road
London NW1 3BH

www.headline.co.uk
www.hodderheadline.com

In memory of
John Thaw 1942–2002

Contents

Preface and Acknowledgements 12

Prologue 15

Dons and Quadrangles 25

Pubs and Hotels 47

Old Oxford and New Murders 73

Literary Mysteries 107

Investigating
Oxfordshire   131

Morse Further
Afield   163

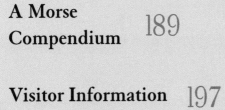

A Morse
Compendium   189

Visitor Information   197

Picture Credits   219

Index   220

Preface and Acknowledgements

JOHN KEATS ONCE WROTE, 'A fact is not a truth until you love it.' The character of Morse – and the world he inhabits – is of course fictional, but his portrayal is so truthful, so honest, that not since Conan Doyle's consulting detective has the public so enthusiastically accepted a literary creation as 'real'.

In his book *The World of Inspector Morse*, Christopher Bird warns us not to be hoodwinked by Morse's Oxford – 'The worlds of all good novels, however realistic they may seem, are creations...his Oxford is not the 'real' Oxford.'

The millions of Morse fans worldwide would disagree. So too, would the thousands from Britain and abroad who each year make the journey to the university city, to walk the same streets as Morse, drink real ale in the same pubs, enter the same college portals and discover firsthand how accurate and well researched the novels are.

The thirteen Morse novels and associated short stories published between 1975 and 1999 are not only Colin Dexter's finest work, but British detective fiction at its zenith.

At 8 p.m. on Tuesday, 6 January 1987 – by coincidence, Sherlock Holmes' 'birthday' – British television viewers were given their first chance to share Dexter's creation. Since then, a staggering 750 million people around the world in more than forty countries have, year by year, come to love the melancholy, sensitive, vulnerable, independent, ungracious, mean-pocketed Morse.

There have been thirty-three television episodes of *Morse*, most filmed in and around Oxford. Although Colin Dexter provided detailed story lines for – and made cameo appearances in – several of these films, only by reading his original novels can you discover the 'real' Inspector Morse country. Dexter's written fiction has, therefore, remained the prime source for this work.

The enjoyment of the Morse mysteries is so personal, so intimate, a pleasure that I have striven to keep the fiction and fascination of Colin Dexter's original books alive by never giving away either the plot or the solution. Characters are mentioned and incidents retold simply to allow the places and the geography in which they occur to be described. The conversations and words used in the text have all been 'spoken' by Morse.

Inspector Morse Country could not have been written without the help of a great many people. It is impossible to measure their contributions. While some contributed greater parts of a chapter, others confirmed a date or location or provided a sentence.

My special gratitude must go to Colin Dexter for granting permission to use extracts from his novels and short stories. I must also thank Sarah Berry, my assistant and secretary and friend; Jane Judd, my loyal and forgiving agent; and Lindsay Symons at Hodder Headline whose inspiration this book was.

Background and reference material came from several publications: *The Oxford of Inspector Morse*, a booklet written by Antony Richards and Philip Attwell for the Inspector Morse Society and published by Irregular Special Press; *The World of Inspector Morse* by Christopher Bird, published by Boxtree; *The Making of Inspector Morse* by Mark Sanderson, published by Macmillan; and *Insight Guides: Oxford*, published by Apa Publications. All authors and publishers readily allowed me to quote from their works.

My gratitude also goes to the following people whom I had the pleasure of interviewing during my research, or with whom I corresponded: Janet Malcolmson, Senior Media and Public Relations Officer with Thames Valley Police; Des Scholes, for his memories and background material on Stamford; Stella McIntyre, Curator of the Royal Signals Museum, Dorset; Philip Mason-Gordon and Rachel Horner at the Old Parsonage Hotel, Oxford; Kizzie at The Randolph Hotel, Oxford; and Nick Simmonds at the Bay Hotel, Lyme Regis.

I have attempted to trace or contact the authors of material published on the Internet. Copyright holders who allowed me to quote from their pages or benefit from their research include: Oxfordshire County Council; Oxford City Council; *Jericho Echo*, and Oxford University.

Every effort was made to trace and seek permission from those holding the copyright to material used in this book. My deepest apologies to anyone I may have inadvertently omitted. Any omissions or errors in the form of credit given that are brought to my or the publisher's attention will be corrected in future printings.

Cliff Goodwin,
2002

Prologue

'FOR MOST PEOPLE, Oxford is synonymous with a few cramped acres that provide the theme of guidebook, novel, poem and film,' Oxfordshire County Council explains, with only a passing reference to Inspector Morse. 'But Oxford belongs to the world and there are times when the world seems to be beating a path to its door.'

It wasn't always so. In fact, Stone Age man did his best to avoid this low-lying spot where two fast-flowing rivers converged. Popular history has it that Oxford acquired its name from a spot on the Thames shallow enough to allow cattle herders to cross with their beasts. Oxen-ford was never a place to loiter, more an exposed and dangerous location, convenient but to be passed through as quickly as possible. The Romans, who never settled near fords and avoided heavy clay soil, were equally unimpressed. They built their villas and their roads to the north and east well above the flood plain.

It was left to the Saxons, who travelled by water and lived on its shores, to lay Oxford's historic foundations. Since the Thames formed a frontier between two Anglo-Saxon kingdoms – Wessex and Mercia – it was inevitable that a natural crossing place should attract a settlement. Locating that first steep-banked and stone-lined river crossing has not been easy. The balance of current thinking puts it at the southern end of St Aldate's, somewhere near where the Folly Bridge now stands.

The Saxons were skilful tacticians and made ample use of the two rivers that merged just beyond the ford. Separating the Thames to the west and the Cherwell to the east was a flat gravel spit, and it is here – beneath what is now Christ Church Meadow – that myth and history eddy.

*Carfax tower is all that remains of the
heart of medieval Oxford*

By AD 635, St Birinus had proclaimed himself Bishop of Dorchester and saw it as part of his divine destiny to convert the Thames Valley to Christianity. His missionaries swept north and decided, in their wisdom, to build a religious community a few hundred yards north of the Thames crossing. What little we know of this holy staging post comes from its obituary rather than any day-to-day records. Its first abbess was St Frideswide, long dead by 1002 when the priory was attacked and burnt to the ground by a Danish raiding party and its monks and nuns massacred. St Frideswide's body survived that onslaught but mysteriously disappeared during the turmoil of the Reformation in the sixteenth century. With the physical evidence gone, romantic legend took over, and the devout and hard-working nun suddenly became endowed with magical and spiritual powers. Born a Mercian princess, her beauty soon attracted the attention of a lecherous royal suitor. To escape his unwanted attentions the pious Frideswide escaped to Oxford and took up holy orders. Undaunted, her would-be lover followed her south. On the eve of snatching Frideswide away, so the story goes, he was struck blind and only the nun's prayers allowed him to regain his sight.

After the attack, enter Edward the Elder of Wessex. The Saxon king surveyed the devastated priory and the ruins of the nearby settlement and decided to become the first town planner in English history. Instead of fortifying the original site, Edward built a completely new town. Surviving street plans of this new Oxford show a planned or 'planted' town with the main streets deliberately laid out within a fortified enclosure. Each building plot was quickly snapped up by merchants and craftsmen who recognised the advantages of living under royal protection. In fact, the town was deemed so safe, and its commercial status was so secure, that it was not long before a mint was located there.

By the time the Normans fought their way ashore near Hastings, Oxford was one of the largest towns in England. The scattered dwellings along the banks of the River Cherwell had been enclosed within a new stone wall. Inside there were about a thousand houses and eleven churches.

Royalty took a liking to this bustling, well-educated town surrounded by acres of well-stocked forest. Henry I built a royal residence outside the city wall, at the west end of today's Beaumont Street, somewhere near where the Ashmolean Museum now stands. It was here that Richard the Lion-Heart was born and possibly King John.

The town, or more correctly the nearby river, played its own small part in determining England's royal line. When Henry I died in 1135, the throne was contested by his daughter, Empress Matilda of Germany, and Stephen Blois. In the fighting that followed, Matilda retreated to Oxford. For three bitterly cold and snowy months, the besieged Empress refused to concede the crown. She finally escaped across the ice-covered Thames camouflaged in a white sheet and Stephen reigned for the next nineteen years.

Little of medieval Oxford remains. An acute and highly tuned imagination is needed to 'walk' the old streets – more than four metres below today's road level – and through the acrid, steamy air of its tanneries, or the musty, dry atmosphere that seemed to envelope its scores of cloth makers.

The heart of old Oxford was at Carfax, derived from the Latin *quadri-furcus* (four-forked), where the medieval streets met in a chaotic and noisy cross-roads. All that remains of the city's ancient centre is the seventeenth-century clock tower of St Martin's Church. Climbing Carfax tower is probably the only excursion in Oxford where you can be sure of not following in Morse's footsteps:

> To his left he noticed that the door of Carfax tower stood open, and beside it a
> notice inviting tourists to ascend and enjoy a panoramic view of Oxford. At the top
> of the tower he could see four or five people standing against the skyline and
> pointing to some of the local landmarks, and a teenaged youth actually sitting on
> the edge, with one of his boots wedged against the next parapet. Morse, feeling a
> twinge of panic somewhere in his bowels, lowered his eyes and walked on.

What had started as a mutual association between the city and its colleges slowly solidified into a vital partnership. No matter how bad the intake or economy of the University, there was always work for the town's folk. By the eighteenth century, almost a quarter of Oxford's residents were employed or studying at the University, and almost all the remainder earned a living housing, feeding or producing the accessories and distractions of student life.

Oxford would always remain famous for the quality of its gloves and cutlery, but not until the early years of the twentieth century would engineering and industry overtake the University as a source of jobs. In the intervening 200 years, the city's economy remained in an academic stranglehold.

A 1721 chronicler noted that 'Oxford daily increases in fine clothes and buildings: never were bricklayers, carpenters and periwig-makers better encouraged there'. Demand from the University for luxury goods also increased the number of clock and watch and scientific instrument makers as well as jewellers and gunsmiths.

Five years later, Daniel Defoe published a series of thirteen 'circuits or journies' entitled *A Tour Through the Whole Island of Great Britain*. It was a work brimming with patriotic optimism and attempted to show the British a vision of their own grandeur. In 'Letter VI', Defoe arrives at Oxford:

> Oxford; the greatest (if not the most
> ancient) university in this island of Great-
> Britain [sic]; and perhaps the most
> flourishing at this time, in men of polite
> learning, and in the most accomplish'd
> masters, in all sciences, and in all the parts
> of acquir'd knowledge in the world... The
> city itself is large, strong, populous, and
> rich; and as it [is] adorn'd by the most
> beautiful buildings of the colleges, and
> halls, it makes the most noble figure of any
> city of its bigness in Europe.

An eighteenth-century view of Oxford High Street – The High – showing All Souls and Queen's Colleges and St Mary's Church

The city was awash with money and good intentions and a rage for improvement. As time went by, the final shadows cast by medieval Oxford were lost in the glare of its newly lit streets. The north and east city gates were demolished and Magdalen Bridge rebuilt.

Hardly had the new bridge been completed when the Great Western Railway announced its intention to build a terminus nearby. Town and Gown were horrified. The University, worried about discipline, and the city traders, concerned about competition

The John Radcliffe Hospital's 'not unpleasing
architecture' dominates Headington Hill

from London, fought off the railway for almost seven years. In 1844, when Oxford was eventually added to the national network, it was by a branch line to nearby Didcot.

The railways created the tourist, and pretty soon the tour guide, and a new breed of traveller began to arrive in Oxford, the forerunners of John Ashenden's little group in *The Jewel That Was Ours*:

> 'Here we are, St Giles'... You can see the plane trees on either side of us, ablaze with the beautiful golden tints of autumn – and, on the left here, St John's College – and Balliol just beyond. And here in front of us, the famous Martyrs' Memorial, modelled on the Eleanor Crosses of Edward the First, and designed by Gilbert Scott to honour the great Protestant martyrs...'

Tourism, Oxford's ultimate saviour, was a long time coming. Throughout Victoria's reign, the University Press remained Oxford's biggest employer. Generations of other workers had little choice but to queue for work outside Lucy's Ironworks, one of the city's two clothing factories or its collection of small breweries. It would take another ninety years – and the vision of one man – for the barometer of Oxford's survival to swing from mental to manual labour.

William Morris, later Lord Nuffield, built and sold his first motor car in 1912. The following year he transferred his business from a cramped city centre garage to a former military training college at Cowley. To keep pace with the nation's love affair with the internal combustion engine, Morris took on more men – 10,000 by the end of the 1930s.

Today, Oxford houses one of the largest medical complexes in Europe. The city's most famous hospital is the John Radcliffe. In *The Silent World of Nicholas Quinn*, Colin Dexter describes its not unpleasing architecture:

> Few of the buildings erected in Oxford since the end of the Second World War have met with much approval from either Town or Gown. Perhaps it is to be expected that a public privileged with the daily sight of so many old and noble buildings should feel a natural prejudice against the reinforced concrete of the curious post-war structures; or perhaps all modern architects are mad. But it is generally agreed that the John Radcliffe Hospital on Headington Hill is one of the least offensive examples of the modern design... The seven-storeyed hospital, built in gleaming off-white brick, its windows painted chocolate brown, is set in spacious, tree-lined grounds, where royal-blue notice boards in bold white lettering direct the strangers towards their destinations.

It would be wrong to dismiss the scientific, political and cultural achievements of Oxford's University graduates as much as it would the city's historic buildings and tourist sights. But for millions of fans, Oxford has a new and fascinating claim to fame. After twenty-four years, thirteen novels and thirty-three television specials, Chief Inspector Morse has investigated almost eighty suspicious deaths – making Oxford the murder capital of Europe.

Dons and Quadrangles

> If, however, you are fond of him and pity him,
> let him indeed fall by the hand of Patroclus,
> but as soon as the life is gone out of him, send
> Death and sweet Sleep to bear him off the
> field and take him to the broad lands of Lycia,
> where his brothers and his kinsmen will bury
> him with mound and pillar, in due honour to
> the dead.
>
> *ILIAD* BOOK XVI

EACH YEAR, Oxford's latest intake of students are introduced to an old joke. It concerns an American tourist who, after wandering around the town for several hours, finally stops an undergraduate and asks directions to the University.

It is a fair question. Oxford does not have a central university campus. What it does have – like that 'other place', Cambridge – is an impressive assortment of city-centre buildings and colleges collectively known as 'the University'.

But that same tourist, walking down Broad Street, might notice an unusual set of railings jutting out into the road. These traditionally separate the 'town' from the 'gown'. That is the key. It is the side from which you approach the problem that makes the difference.

To the majority of Oxford residents and non-academics, the separation is physical; the University can be touched and pointed at. Yet to those who are taught or who teach there, or who are employed by it, the University is a more nebulous establishment. It is, but it isn't.

'Perhaps,' Morse says in *The Secret of Annexe 3*, 'it was the masks that were the reality, and the faces beneath them that were the pretence.' He is talking himself through a murder. He could equally be attempting to explain the complexities of the University and its staff.

Unlike his creator, who obtained a classics degree at Cambridge, Morse failed his finals. It left him with a deep sense of forever being on the steps of the University, invited in for special occasions but always shown the door afterwards. 'This,' explains Dexter, 'may account for some of the cynical and cruel judgements he makes upon it.' Environmental studies, he doubted, was little more than a euphemism for occasional visits to the gasworks, the fire station and the sewage installations, while for sociology and sociologists he had nothing but sour contempt... With such a plethora of non-subjects crowding the timetable, there was no room for the traditional disciplines.

Where Dexter presents us with wonderfully obnoxious and objectionable academics such as Sir Clixby Bream in *Death is Now My Neighbour*, only films such as *Twilight of the Gods* or *The Settling of the Sun* show us the University in full pompous flood. And what a confusing and privileged world it is. Each independently governed college has a head who is variously titled the Rector, Master, Principal, President, Warden or Provost. The lecturers or teachers are called dons, although not all dons teach, and members of the cleaning and housekeeping staff are known as scouts. Christ Church, which features in *Who Killed Harry Field?*, is popularly known as 'the House'. It does not have students in the traditional sense, that label being reserved for its dons.

It is difficult to find one of the thirty-five colleges listed on the Oxford University Register that has not been mentioned in a Morse novel or appeared, even momentarily, in one of the television episodes – University and Merton Colleges in *The Infernal Serpent*, New College in *Fat Chance*, and Magdalen College in *Dead on Time, Twilight of the Gods* and *The Dead of Jericho*.

To this, Colin Dexter and the scriptwriters have added their own thinly disguised educational settings – Wolsey College in *The Daughters of Cain*, St Saviour's in *Fat Chance*, Beaumont in *The Last Enemy,* and Courtenay in *Ghost in the Machine.* There is one fictional college Dexter relies on more than most – Lonsdale.

But it was a real college the young Morse attended. The Oxford into which he was plunged as a twenty-year-old must have been an exciting but confusing place. He was still attempting to understand it fifty years later. Morse's National Service was over and in October 1950 – while the rest of Britain appeared preoccupied with the depressing news from Korea – he arrived in Oxford for his first term as an undergraduate at St John's College.

St John's College gateway, through which Morse first entered the college as an undergraduate in the early 1950s

The university city of Oxford was busy this morning, the third full day of the Michaelmas term. First-year undergraduates, with spankingly new college scarves tossed over their shoulders, eagerly exploring the bookshops of the Broad, and a trifle self-consciously strode down the High into the crowded Cornmarket...and thence, according to taste, into the nearest pubs and coffee shops.

At Oxford, it was his flat, Lincolnshire accent that attracted the attention of his fellow undergraduates who promptly nicknamed him 'Paganus' – from the Latin for rustic or villager – which was very soon shortened to 'Pagan'. To his friends and the college authorities, he insisted on being known simply as 'Morse'.

For two years Morse was the clichéd model student – he rarely skipped a lecture, worked conscientiously at his texts, was always prompt with his unseens and compositions, and – as predicted – gained a First in Classical Moderations.

Third year undergraduates at St John's were expected to vacate their rooms and move into various college-owned properties. Returning to Oxford in the autumn of 1952, Morse was informed he would be lodging at No. 24 St John Street.

Running south from Wellington Square and exiting on to Beaumont Street not far from the Ashmolean Museum, St John Street was built by St John's College as a speculative development in the 1820s. By its completion three years into Queen Victoria's reign, the design of its Georgian terraces was already beginning to look dated.

Morse settled into his new surroundings and innocently focused on his 'Greats', unaware of the emotional whirlwind about to engulf him.

In late February the following year, Morse attended an Oxford University Drama Society production of 'Doctor

St John Street where Morse lived as an
undergraduate in the early 1950s

Faustus' at a small theatre in Beaumont Street. During the interval he met and 'impetuously' fell in love with a postgraduate student who, he was surprised to learn, had recently taken a room next door to his own digs at No. 22 St John Street. His affair with Wendy Spencer lasted exactly a year:

> Their days and weeks and months were spent in long, idyllic happiness: they walked together across the Oxfordshire countryside; went to theatres, cinemas, concerts, museums; spent much time in pubs and restaurants; and, after a while, much time in bed together, too.

At the end of the 1953 Trinity term, Morse was abruptly warned by his classics tutor, Dr Browne-Smith, that he was in grave danger of failing his finals. Wendy Spencer's supervisor at St Hilda's College was less tolerant. Just after Christmas she was informed her doctorate grant had been suspended. Determined, but still distracted, the pair continued their studies, Morse attempting to cut down on his consumption of beer and read the occasional book while Wendy funded her final months at university by working as a part-time waitress at The Randolph Hotel.

Their resolution lasted until the second week in February. Called home to visit her widowed stroke-victim mother, Wendy never returned to Oxford. In the 'dark weeks and dark letters' that followed, Morse came to realise her excuses for staying away – the family were desperately short of money and she was duty bound to help – only devalued and disarmed his owns pleas for a reunion.

Twice he visited her West Country home without success. By April his St John's tutors lost patience and his college grant was withdrawn. The humiliation of having to apply to Lincolnshire County Council for a top-up grant never left him. And then, three weeks before his 'Greats', the final letter from Wendy Spencer arrived. It was over.

Morse remained in Oxford 'doing nothing, absolutely nothing' until his results were posted. In his head he kept repeating the advice he had first seen written in coloured silks and displayed on the wall of a Maidstone bed and breakfast establishment:

If you love her, set her free
If she loves you, she will gladly return to you
If she doesn't she never really loved you anyway

That summer Morse left Oxford 'a withdrawn and silent young man, bitterly belittled, yet not completely broken in spirit'. He had failed his *Literae Humaniores* and now faced the prospect of breaking the news to his ailing father.

During the day, Morse would walk the countryside around Stamford – up to Easton-on-the-Hill or off to Tinwell or Burghley Park or north into the woodlands between Stamford and Grantham and Bourne. It was his father, a month or two before his death, who suggested his only son might find a 'niche' somewhere in the police force.

In *The Riddle of the Third Mile*, Colin Dexter allows his hero a brief moment of hope and panic. Morse was in London and on his way to a house in Putney where a woman with the initials W.S. lived – 'The name Wendy Spencer tripped trochoidally across his brain... It couldn't be the same woman. It *wasn't* the same woman. And yet, ye gods – if gods ye be – please make it her!'

Despite his failure as a student, Morse owed a great deal to his former college. Unlike the army, where he was just another number, perhaps for the first time in his life St John's gave him a sense of belonging; he was part of a great and wealthy tradition, but always an individual.

Morse's old college is claimed to be the wealthiest in the city. This exceptional wealth has always meant lavish buildings for its Fellows and secure and luxurious accommodation for its 350 students. University fable has it that you can walk all the way from Oxford to Cambridge on land owned by St John's. Founded in 1555, its many assets include extensive parts of London's West End and even numerous acres of Swiss countryside.

Situated on St Giles' – which it also owns – St John's is academically the most consistently successful of all the Oxford colleges. Among its distinguished alumni are Philip Larkin, Robert Graves, Kingsley Amis and Morse's hero of poetry, A.E. Housman.

The site of St John's campus was originally occupied by a college founded by Archbishop Chichele in 1437 for the education of Cistercian monks, and named in honour of St Bernard. Its work ended with the dissolution of the monasteries. After years of dereliction it was rebuilt and refounded by Sir Thomas White.

Unlike the guided tourists, it would have taken Morse several days – possibly weeks – to notice the statue occupying the niche on the inside of St John's gate tower. Commissioned in the mid-1930s, Eric Gill's portrayal of St John the Baptist is a belated recognition of the college's 1555 renaming by White, elected Mayor of London in 1546 and a member of the Merchant Taylor's Guild. The prophet is the patron saint of tailors.

It is not only generations of students who have benefited from White's philanthropy. In his will he bequeathed the sum of £1,400 for the purchase of lands, the revenues from which were to be advanced by way of interest-free loans to young men 'of fair name and fame' under the age of thirty-five, to enable them to commence, or help them in, business. Five towns were covered by the bequest, the money rotating annually between Leicester, Coventry, Northampton, Warwick and Nottingham. The charity is still in existence, with each city now able to lend between £300,000 and £400,000 a year. Interest-free loans are given to young people to establish a business or to help with their education.

*St John's College's coat of arms includes a lamb and flag which is the name of
a nearby public house favoured by college students in the 1880s*

Thirty years on from Morse's first encounter with his St John's classics tutor, the
ponderously named Dr Oliver Maximilian Alexander Browne-Smith had moved from St
John's to Lonsdale College. When, in *The Riddle of the Third Mile*, a grammatically
suspicious note – 'You mean he'd have put commas after "sudden" – and "through"?' – is
delivered to the Master of Lonsdale purporting to have been written by Browne-Smith, it
is Morse who is asked to investigate.

Within Morse's jurisdiction, Lonsdale appears to be the most licentious and murderous of
Oxford's thirty-five colleges. In *The Way Through the Woods*, the Chief Inspector attends a
Lonsdale concert and starts another hopeful yet doomed relationship, this time with Clare
Osborne, before returning to the college to question lecturer and pornography aficionado, Dr
Alan Hardinge. Another academic, Dr Bernard Crowther, falls under suspicion in *Last Bus
to Woodstock*, as do the sanguinary Dr and Mrs Storrs in *Death is Now My Neighbour*. In *The*

Dead of Jericho, Catherine Edgerley is an undergraduate at Lonsdale, and in *The Riddle of the Third Mile*, Morse's own university career becomes murderously entwined with college politics.

In reality, Lonsdale does not exist. No doubt attracted by its rebellious history and Lincolnshire ancestry, Colin Dexter admits that much of Lonsdale's 'history and traditions' was inspired by Brasenose College. The evolution of the University, as we shall see, is peppered with intrigue and violence, but for centuries of internal strife and scandal, Brasenose is hard to beat.

There is little doubt that medieval Brasenose Hall took its name from the heavy, brass-coloured knocker attached to its main gate. Its presence, and that of the college, was first recorded in 1279. Colleges, like churches, were places of refuge for thirteenth-century outlaws and villains. All that was needed was to place a hand on the door of a college for the fugitive to be granted entry and temporary refuge.

Brasenose's attachment to its knocker did not last long. A group of disillusioned fourteenth-century students unbolted and stole the knocker before fleeing to Stamford in Lincolnshire – Morse's birthplace – with the intention of establishing a rival university. Edward II refused to endorse the new institution and the rebel students eventually drifted back to Oxford or settled in Cambridge. The 'brass nose' was somehow forgotten and left in Lincoln where an opportunistic builder attached it to one of his latest developments, appropriately called Brasenose House.

Back in Oxford, a succession of at least ten halls occupied and vacated the Brasenose site, among them Burwaldescote, Amsterdam, St Thomas's Hall, Sheld Hall, Ivy Hall, Little University Hall, Salysurry Hall and Little Edmund Hall.

Various attempts to return the original bronze knocker to its rightful home all failed and a new knocker was made, this time in the shape of a human head, and placed at the apex of the college gate. When Brasenose House in Stamford finally came on the market in 1890, yet another effort was made to retrieve the relic. The owner was prepared to sell – but only for the price of the entire house. The original knocker now hangs behind the high table in the college dining hall.

In 1509, the Bishop of Lincoln, William Smythe, joined forces with Richard Sutton, a wealthy and philanthropic lawyer, to establish the surviving Brasenose College. Finding benefactors for Brasenose was not hard and for almost a hundred years the college flourished, notably under the principalship of Alexander Nowell who, much to Morse's delight, is credited with the invention of bottled beer.

By the early decades of the seventeenth century, things had changed. With the autocratic Principal Radcliffe governing the college, successive financial scandals rippled just below the surface. The most troublesome concerned a group of fretful Junior Fellows who claimed their income was seriously out of ratio with their more senior colleagues. In 1643 things came to a

head when the lecturers petitioned Charles I to command a visitation – a kind of parliamentary audit. Unfortunately, Parliament was a little preoccupied at the time and it wasn't until the end of the Civil War that the Brasenose accounts were finally scrutinised and Principal Radcliffe deposed.

With its main gate opposite the gracious and proudly independent Radcliffe Camera, completed in 1748 and funded from the estate of the royal surgeon Dr John Radcliffe to house a science and medicine library, the college's old quad presents an outstanding collection of Tudor buildings.

Originally completed for Brasenose's 1509 foundation, the third floor of dormer windows was added in the early seventeenth century. Still more eye-catching is the blue-and-white sundial painted in 1719 on the eastern quad wall. Look higher still and a strange collection of Gothic pinnacles and Baroque urns decorate the parapets – competing with the anachronistic statue of a rugby player on the college's High Street frontage.

The list of Brasenose alumni includes an impressive number of legal, military and literary figures: Lord Scarman, John Mortimer, Field Marshal Earl Haig, John Buchan, Jeffrey Archer, William Golding and the television personality and writer Michael Palin.

One with whom Morse would have felt particularly comfortable was Robert Burton, the author of *The Anatomy of Melancholy*, and a book the Chief Inspector himself reads while at

Brasenose College – overshadowed by the Radcliffe Camera – becomes Lonsdale College in several of the Morse novels

*The stunning eighteenth-century sundial on
the eastern wall of Brasenose quad*

home and bedridden during *The Daughters of Cain* investigation.

There is, however, a more sinister side to university life – the deadly and highly contagious Oxford disease. As a sufferer, it is a condition Morse knows only too well. The symptoms surface in almost all of Colin Dexter's books, but it is left to Sheila Williams in *The Jewel That Was Ours* to quantify its effects as that 'tragic malady which deludes its victims into believing they can never be wrong in any matter of knowledge or opinion'.

Only in the television episodes are the vitriolic and pettifogging minds of the university élite laid bare. Oxford, claims Deborah Burns in *The Last Enemy*, is 'a vicious, backbiting, petty-minded, parochial little town that thinks it's the centre of the universe'.

And in the television adaptation of *Death is Now My Neighbour*, the Master of Lonsdale, Sir Clixby Bream, admits to the wife of a potential successor: 'The dons are malicious, spiteful creatures. They don't vote for someone, they vote against them. That's why they'll vote against Denis, even though he is the best man for the job... He's let them know how much he wants it.'

For Morse, at least, it was easy to identify a fellow sufferer. Theodore Kemp MA, D.Phil. (Oxon), now Keeper of Anglo-Saxon and Medieval Antiquities at Oxford's Ashmolean Museum, was just such a man. The pair meet for the first time in *The Jewel That Was Ours*:

> Almost immediately Kemp slotted into Morse's preconceptions of the we-are-an-Oxford-man... The bearded, clever-looking, ugly-attractive man who sat down only after lightly dusting the seat with a hyper-handkerchief...another person might have been irritated only temporarily by the man's affected lisp. Not so Morse.

The Oxford disease is nothing new. It was rampant more than 250 years ago. Matthew Arnold, whose poetry immortalised Oxford as 'that sweet city of dreaming spires', hinted at it in a letter to his mother written in 1861: 'The intellectual life here is certainly much

Merton College where the garden scenes for the television episode The Infernal Serpent *were filmed*

more intense than it used to be; but this place has its disadvantages too, in the envies, hatreds, and jealousies that come with the activity of mind of most men.'

A century earlier, Adam Smith in *Wealth of Nations* dismissed Oxford as a 'sanctuary in which exploded systems and obsolete prejudices find shelter and protection long after they have been hunted out of every corner of the world'.

George Bernard Shaw's diagnosis was more sarcastic: 'It is characteristic of the authorities that they should consider a month too little for the preparation of a boat race, and grudge three weeks to the rehearsals of one of Shakespeare's plays.'

In the television episode *The Settling of the Sun*, based on a Colin Dexter story line, the Master of Lonsdale repeats possibly the oldest Oxford joke of all – '... for the members of the University as a whole. And, gentlemen, what a hole Oxford is!'

It is certainly centuries older than a lot of the colleges that collectively make up Oxford University, many of which have been used as centrepieces or backdrops for the *Morse* television episodes. But tracing the origins of the oldest English-speaking university in the world is not easy. There was no individual founder, only a group of audiences, but teaching took place in Oxford as early as the start of the eleventh century. By 1200 the city had acquired a reputation for legal learning and, once its first chancellor was elected, quickly won royal and episcopal support.

For most of the Middle Ages, the unobservant traveller might pass through Oxford without noticing there was a university at all. Principal meetings and ceremonies were held in the church of St Mary the Virgin and lectures given in hired venues. Three colleges – University, Balliol and Merton – were founded in the thirteenth century, with several more in the late Middle Ages. All comprised a small and privileged minority of Fellows.

Merton College – founded in 1264, by Walter de Merton to train graduates for careers in the church, medicine and the law – claims to be the oldest Oxford college. Famous graduates include Thomas Bodley, the founder of the Bodleian Library; Lord Randolph Churchill, Sir Winston Churchill's father; T.S. Eliot; and the musician and actor Kris Kristofferson.

The college's Fellows' Garden, off Merton Street, was used as the garden location for the fictional Beaufort College in the television investigation *The Infernal Serpent*.

Oxford's first academic halls were ordinary large town houses rented by masters who used them for both teaching and to provide shelter for their students. In *The Miller's Tale*, Geoffrey Chaucer describes the living conditions of Nicholas, a wealthy Oxford student, who lodged with a prosperous carpenter. His private chamber contained a bed, a shelf of books, musical and scientific instruments, a bow and arrow, food and drink, and much jewellery.

Violence was commonplace, not only between scholars and townsmen but even between students from different areas of the city. The most notorious Town–Gown riot was on St Scholastica's Day – 10 February – 1355. What began as a tavern brawl quickly led to the sacking of several halls in which six clerks were killed and dozens of other people injured. From then until 1825, the mayor and burgesses of Oxford were obliged to attend the Church of St Mary the Virgin each year on St Scholastica's Day for an 'humiliating' ceremony, during which 60 pence – one for each of the original burgesses – was handed over to the University.

Another very ancient college, founded little more than twenty years after the St Scholastica's Day massacre, is New College. Established to train

New College dates from 1379 and its magnificent chapel is featured in Fat Chance

replacement priests quickly, after the extensive depopulation of clerics during the Black Death, it was the first college to accept both undergraduates and graduates. The church service that opens *Fat Chance* was filmed in its fourteenth-century chapel. Famous old boys include the left-wing politician Tony Benn and the novelists John Galsworthy and John Fowles.

When Henry VIII dissolved the monasteries and friaries, much of the church's Oxford property was handed over to the city's colleges. The most notable beneficiary was Christ Church, built by Cardinal Wolsey on the site of St Frideswide's, whose rich endowments included the entire possessions of Osney Abbey.

Christ Church has maintained its place as the largest and most famous of Oxford colleges and three television episodes of *Morse – The Daughters of Cain, Last Seen Wearing* and *The Secret of Bay 5B* – were filmed both in and outside the college. One of the college's ancient – and confusing – eccentricities provides Morse with a vital clue in *The Daughters of Cain* – the dons are colloquially known as Students rather than Fellows.

Within the college walls is Christ Church Cathedral, the smallest cathedral in Britain. The college's famous Tom Tower gets its name from the seven-ton bell, Great Tom, taken from the twelfth-century Osney Abbey, which tolls a 101 times at 9.05 every evening – in theory, the time by which Oxford's students are meant to be in bed.

Traditionally, Christ Church, once known as Cardinal College after its founder, is one of the most aristocratic colleges. Fourteen British prime ministers studied there, including Lord Liverpool, George Canning, Sir Robert Peel, William Gladstone and Anthony Eden. Among its literary graduates are Charles Dodgson (Lewis Carroll, the author of *Alice in Wonderland*), Auberon Waugh and W.H. Auden. William Penn, the founder of Pennsylvania, also studied there.

Oxford University spent much of the eighteenth century in defensive decline but there was one area in which the University excelled – architecture. No matter how low the student intake fell, Oxford continued to embellish its streets with impressive buildings. One college, Queen's, was completely rebuilt and twelve of the other eighteen were altered. The enormous expenditure was designed, at least in part, to encourage the return of those frightened off by the University's staid and stale reputation.

With Queen Victoria on the throne, great changes were taking place within the University. In *The Silent World of Nicholas Quinn*, Colin Dexter gives his own history lesson:

*Christ Church Cathedral is unique in being both a college chapel
and the smallest cathedral in England*

Christ Church on which Wolsey College
in The Daughters of Cain *is based*

By the middle of the nineteenth century radical reforms were afoot in Oxford; and by its end a series of Commissions, Statutes, and Parliamentary Bills had inaugurated changes which were to transform the life of both Town and Gown. The University syllabuses were extended to include the study of the emergent sciences, and of modern history; the high academic standards set by Benjamin Jowett's Balliol gradually spread to other colleges; the establishment of professorial chairs increasingly attracted to Oxford scholars of international renown; the secularization of the college fellowships began to undermine the traditionally religious framework of university discipline and administration; and young men of Romanist, Judaic, and other strange persuasions were now admitted as undergraduates.

An association for the Higher Education of Women at Oxford was established and, within fifteen years, four women's colleges were opened: Lady Margaret Hall (1878), Somerville

(1879), St Hugh's (1886) and St Hilda's (1893), where Morse's lover Wendy Spencer later studied. Although the female undergraduates sat university examinations, they were not formally awarded degrees until 1920.

From the middle of the nineteenth century, student numbers began to rise and the second building programme in 200 years got under way. Balliol and Exeter colleges were almost entirely rebuilt. New colleges were founded. Keble College was built between 1868 and 1882 to commemorate John Keble, a founder of the High Church Oxford Movement in the 1830s. Designed by William Butterfield, it was controversially the first college to be built in brick.

Oxford student life in the final quarter of the nineteenth century was dominated by a changing world and still faster changing social attitudes. One Magdalen College undergraduate who still found the capacity to shock was the poet and future dramatist, Oscar Wilde – full name Oscar Fingal O'Flahertie Wills Wilde. He transferred to Oxford after studying at Trinity College in his native Dublin. Despite his flamboyant and outrageous behaviour and exotic lifestyle, he had a great head for hard work and obtained first-class degrees. In his *Oxford Notebooks*, Wilde recalls his university years as:

> …days of lyrical ardour and of studious sonnet-writing; days when one loved
> the exquisite intricacy and musical repetitions of the ballade, and villanelle with
> its linked long-drawn echoes and its curious completeness; days when one
> solemnly sought to discover the proper temper in which a triolet should be
> written; delightful days, in which, I am glad to say, there was far more rhyme
> than reason.

The twenty-three-year-old Wilde, already unpopular with the university authorities, was temporarily suspended from Magdalen in 1877 after he was late returning from a vocational visit to Greece. The penalty meant he was no longer allowed to room in college and Wilde moved into the Old Parsonage on the Banbury Road. It is now a luxury hotel, on which the Haworth Hotel in *The Secret of Annexe 3* is based.

The tall, yellow-stone tower of Wilde's old college still dominates the Oxford skyline and features in three *Morse* television stories: *The Dead of Jericho, Dead on Time* and *Twilight of the Gods*. Magdalen's bell tower can also be seen in the film *Shadowlands*, shot at the college where C.S. Lewis was a lecturer. At 6 a.m. on May Day each year, the college's choristers chant madrigals and sing the hymn to spring, '*Te Deum Patrem Colimus*'.

The twentieth century was remarkable for the creation of a number of postgraduate college institutions. Apart from Nuffield, funded largely by the motor magnate of the same name, they include St Antony's College, Linacre College, Wolfson College and Green College.

Magdalen College – featured in the television episodes Twilight of the Gods, Dead on Time *and* The Dead of Jericho *– in a more peaceful age*

One undergraduate college, St Peter's, is a wholly twentieth-century foundation and two others, St Anne's and St Catherine's, originated as nineteenth-century societies for non-collegiate students. By the 1990s, there were thirty-five colleges, plus six permanent private halls founded by religious denominations. In term time, more than 10,000 undergraduates and postgraduates study or work at Oxford University.

But it was to an earlier university expansion, and a slackening of the colleges' strict social code, that Morse owed something else – the flat to which he retreated to listen to his music and complete his crosswords.

University mythology has it that the area north of the Martyrs' Memorial was first developed when the university authorities gave permission for dons to marry. Large families needed large houses and by 1880 the majority of available sites had been developed. Two years later, the first horse-drawn trams were rattling up the Banbury Road on 4ft-gauge rails. Their passengers were charged a single penny all the way from Carfax. Other Victorian sounds were to be heard, such as the hollow tap of croquet played on summer lawns and the rattle and polite chatter of afternoon tea, served with ceremony. Progressively through the twentieth century, the professors and professionals who inhabited North Oxford gave their élite domain more than an air of exclusivity. The dons in particular spoke with a refined pronunciation which came to be known as 'North Oxford' – the 'o' in college would be pronounced 'u' to be delivered as *cullage*.

One of the reasons why so many people have taken to Morse is that he was unmistakably human; his talents may be unique, but his faults are universal. His home – a bachelor flat in one of those large houses at the far end of a North Oxford cul-de-sac – was, however, exclusively Morse. His only treasured possessions were his complete CD catalogue of every Wagner opera and his collection of A.E. Housman first editions. A reproduction of Vermeer's 'Milkmaid' was one of the few pieces of 'art' Morse owned.

Morse inherited little from his relatives and the only family heirloom he possessed was a nest of 1756 Chippendale tables, stolen and returned in the short story *Neighbourhood Watch*. The lounge, with three walls lined with bookshelves, contained little more than the 'heavy old walnut suite his mother had left him'.

Whenever the mood took him, Morse would sink into the sofa and close his eyes. For almost four decades, the BBC had invited guests to step out of their everyday existence and become castaways, taking with them eight favourite pieces of music and a small selection of 'luxuries'. It was time for Morse to review his own 'Desert Island Discs'. The majority would be Wagner. He had always considered the four operas which made up 'Der Ring des Nibelungen' as one of the seven wonders of the modern world. Perhaps he'd have Kirsten Flagstad singing an extract from 'The Ring' or, better still, something by Gwladys Probert – 'the greatest diva of her time', and the 'Recordare' from Mozart's 'Requiem' (K626), and certainly Richard Strauss's 'melismatic' 'Vier Letzte Lieder'. The eighth record was a worry, though; perhaps he should have 'In Paradisum' from Faure's 'Requiem' instead of the slow movement from Dvorak's 'American Quartet'?

About now the telephone would ring to shatter his concentration. It was usually Lewis.

Pubs and Hotels

Alcoholism: *n.* the mental illness and compulsive behaviour resulting from alcohol dependency

OXFORD ENGLISH DICTIONARY

THE *OXFORD ENGLISH DICTIONARY* defines alcoholism as 'the mental illness and compulsive behaviour resulting from alcohol dependency'. Morse is certainly guilty of compulsive and obsessive behaviour, but how far does his life rely on the contents of a cask of real ale or a tumbler or two of Glenfiddich? Is Morse really an alcoholic?

Historically and clinically, he certainly exhibits most of the symptoms. Morse admits to taking his first taste of beer as a fourteen-year-old schoolboy. As an adult, alcohol has become part of his daily life. He drinks faster and consumes more than anyone else. He finds it difficult to refuse the offer of a drink, even accepting a midday gin and tonic 'just to do the right thing'. And, far more significantly, he believes alcohol improves his performance as a detective.

> Again and again he came so near to cornering that single piece of information –
> something seen? something heard? – that was still so tantalisingly eluding him.
> After his fourth pint, he wondered if he ever would remember it, for he knew
> from long and loving addiction that his brain was never so keen as after beer.

But is it that exquisite state between intoxication and inspiration that Morse desperately needs, or merely the act of drinking? Perhaps it's the feel of a pint glass in his hand, and not the effect of its contents, that he needs.

Counsellors at Gamblers' Anonymous – another vice that Morse has never altogether shaken off – have long claimed it is the act of walking into a bookie's and placing a bet, not the winning or losing, that provides the addictive stimulation. The sense of urgency – the desperation – is the same. 'Nearest pub, Lewis,' Morse orders his sergeant in *The Daughters of Cain*. 'We need to think a little.'

The 'blessedly music – muzak – free environment' of the Turf Tavern where scenes for
Service of All the Dead *and* The Silent World of Nicholas Quinn *were filmed*

Despite the obvious disapproval of his superior, the coffee and chocolate biscuit addicted Superintendent Strange, Morse's drinking habits remain under control. He may arrive for a meeting with the Chief Constable with a whiff of whisky on his breath, but we never see him really drunk. 'The secret of a happy life,' he informs Lewis in *The Silent World of Nicholas Quinn*, 'is to know when to stop and then go that little bit further.'

The Black Prince at Woodstock where Morse and Lewis first join forces in Last Bus to Woodstock

But addicted or not, Morse fails to evade the ultimate fate of all heavy drinkers. In 1994, at the age of sixty-four, his body finally begins to break down. In the middle of *The Daughters of Cain* he suffers a severe bout of bronchitis and is confined first to his own and then to a hospital bed. Asked by Strange, 'What exactly's wrong with you?' Morse rattles off a litany of complaints.

'My liver and kidneys are disintegrating. My blood pressure isn't quite off the top of the scale – not yet; I'm nursing another stomach ulcer, and as if that wasn't enough I'm on the verge of diabetes, because my pancreas, they tell me, isn't producing sufficient insulin to counteract my occasional intake of alcohol. Oh yes, my cholesterol's dangerously high.'

Resolutions to stop smoking and drastically cut his alcohol intake are repeatedly made and broken. His doctor's warnings go unheeded. It is not his own end that occupies Morse, who has other things on his mind...and to make his mind work he needs a drink.

'Death,' Morse confides to Lewis in the television episode *The Sins of the Fathers*, 'always makes people close ranks... Death and money.' The death in question is not only the murder of Trevor Radford, but the corporate smothering of the small family-run Oxford brewery of which he is managing director.

As a student, Morse must surely have drunk his ration of Radford's – 'one of the finest real ales in the country'. He certainly appreciated good beer. Within weeks of his arrival in

1952, Morse had joined SPARTA, a university society dedicated to the promotion (and consumption) of traditional real ale. It was, in many ways, the pre-cursor of CAMRA – the Campaign for Real Ale – of which Colin Dexter was an early member.

Two years national service in the army had left Morse with an abiding dislike of ill-fitting, itchy clothes and a serious and passionate taste for beer. Oxford, with its 700-year history of brewing and its cache of independent brew houses, must have seemed heaven-sent to a twenty-year-old student. But then Oxford, slap in the middle of malting barley country, always did have a head start. If Town and Gown are historically inter-woven, then beer is the flux that binds them.

The Poll Tax of 1381 recorded no fewer than thirty-two professional brewers living within the city boundary. Even then, while the poor begged in the streets and pollution trickled into the Thames, the authorities felt the beer trade was so important it was governed by strict quality control and taxes.

Most colleges had their own brew houses and produced beers of varying, and dubious, potency. In 1600, the President of Trinity College recorded: 'The houses that had the smaller [weaker] beer had the most drunkards, for it forced them to go into the town to comfort their stomachs.' The strongest beer was brewed and sold at All Souls. After a heavy drinking session at Christ Church in 1729, the Keeper of the Ashmolean died 'from a pretty deal of small beer'.

Beer, Morse insisted to Lewis, was 'pure food'

By the time Morse was marking his SPARTA report card, the city's legendary breweries had all but disappeared – Swan's Nest Brewery, down by the river; Hall's Oxford Brewery; St Clement's Brewery; the Eagle Steam Brewery; and Hanley's City Breweries. But his dedication to hand-pumped beer straight from the wood never left him. 'Without being too doctrinaire about what he was prepared to drink,' Colin Dexter explains in *Last Seen Wearing*, 'Morse preferred a flat pint to a fizzy keg most breweries were now serving.'

He wasn't too fussy about the surroundings in which he sipped his pint. Like most drinkers, Morse shared a momentary enjoyment of the view from a pub window or the countryside beyond a beer garden, but the pleasure quickly evaporates as the alcohol takes hold and the serious work of thinking begins. As a foreword to *Death is Now My Neighbour*, Colin Dexter quotes the Greek comic dramatist Aristophanes: 'Quickly, bring me a beaker of wine, so that I may wet my mind and say something clever.'

Few words are devoted to describing a public house or bar in a Morse novel. In *Last Bus to Woodstock*, a mystery centred on the death of a young woman in a pub car park, Dexter expends just thirty-five words on describing the interior of the Black Prince at Woodstock.

> The lounge itself, deeply carpeted, with chairs and wall seats covered in a pleasing orange shade, was gently bathed in half light, giving a chiaroscuro effect reminiscent, it was hoped, of a Rembrandt nativity scene.

It suggests a suitable and pleasing ambiance for a thirsty tourist stopping off after a visit to nearby Blenheim Palace, or even for Lewis on a family day out, but hardly of interest to Morse. Only once do we hear of Morse visiting a pub, more correctly planning to visit a pub, for recreational purposes – and even then it was to exercise his mind and memory.

On the first day of 1986, Morse is feeling suspiciously relaxed. He is about to start two weeks' furlough and 'Die Walküre' is about to engulf his flat with Wagnerian energy. In an hour or so he intends setting off for the nearby Friar pub to play his part in his quiz team's expected victory. When the telephone rings, Morse allows it to ring for several minutes before he finally picks up the receiver.

> 'I suppose you've just staggered out of bed all ready for another night of debauchery?'
>
> 'And a Happy New Year to you, too, Sir.'
>
> 'We've got a murder down at the bottom of your road,' said the Chief Constable. 'I'm assuming you had nothing to do with it, of course.'

The temptation of greater problems to solve than a pub quiz can offer gets the better of him, and a feeble protest is soon overtaken by Sergeant Lewis's appearance outside his boss's North Oxford flat. The pair's arrival a few minutes later at the Haworth Hotel, a little further down the Banbury Road and based on the Old Parsonage Hotel, begins a hotel whodunnit in classic Agatha Christie style. *The Secret of Annexe 3* not only involves the body of a man wearing Rastafarian fancy dress, but an obligatory scattering of red-herrings from a blackmailer, a fornicator, a fraud and a bully among the other guests.

The Old Parsonage is North Oxford's most noted hostelry. It creaks with history and its superbly restored rooms come complete with a resident ghost. Situated between Keble College to the east and Somerville College to the west, and just north of where the tree-lined St Giles' becomes the Banbury Road, it is perhaps the city's most architecturally romantic hotel.

Walking the same route in *Annexe 3*, Colin Dexter approaches the hotel through:

> ... houses built of a cheerful orange-red brick that gives an immediate
> impression of warmth and good fellowship after the slightly forbidding façades
> of the Venetian wedge (between St Giles' and the Woodstock Road). Now the
> roofs are of red tile, and the paintwork around the stone-plinthed windows of
> an almost uniform white.

The site on which the Old Parsonage stands dates back to 1308, around the time when the university colleges first came into being, although a hotel was not established until three-and-a-half centuries later. The building, now a much-loved city landmark, has played its own part in Oxford's history – as a sanctuary for the persecuted clergy from neighbouring St Giles'; as a stronghold for the Royalists during the Civil War; and as a temporary home for numerous literati, including Oscar Wilde.

Until the mid fourteenth century, the priest of a medieval hospice, which had reputedly stood on the site since the Norman Conquest, had his dwelling there, next to St Giles' Church – hence the name Old Parsonage.

Run by nuns for the 'poor and infirm', rent was paid to the church in the form of candles made by the hospice inmates. A bricked-up archway in the present cellar is said to be part of a tunnel connecting the house to St Giles' Church. In times of religious danger, priests and nuns would use the underground escape route – and one sister still does. The ghostly figure of a nun is occasionally seen floating through this part of the house.

Far less mysterious were the dodgy dealings of Edward Selwood, the prosperous chef of nearby St John's College, who appears to have financed his new home on the Old Parsonage site with the proceeds of various dubious enterprises. As a chef, Selwood was a respected member of university society. Bought by University College as an endowment for its early scholars, the methods Selwood used to acquire a lease on the site were rumoured to include blackmail and even attempted murder. Other Selwood scams included bribery, back-handers and the seventeenth-century equivalent of cooking the books.

Master cooks made substantial additions to their wages through gratuities from traders and monetary encouragement from wealthier masters. There was also a good profit to be made from selling surplus food from the college kitchens. But Selwood added a new twist. By the 1630s, he was already running a successful Chop House in Broad Street, which bought the extra provisions he had over-ordered for his university pantry. He was also leasing a farm from another college – from which his St John's kitchens purchased all its meat.

The enterprising chef needed to launder his profits somewhere and in 1640 started work on his new house. He got as far as sub-letting the south part of the present house during the reign of Charles I when the Civil War literally landed on his doorstep.

The Royalist headquarters were based in Oxford and a part of the army's defences was constructed on Old Parsonage land. Despite the flying cannonballs and a hail of musket shot, the building survived the Parliamentarian bombardment without damage, and the house was completed in time to celebrate the restoration of Charles II in 1660.

After various owners and extensions, the Old Parsonage was acquired in 1989 by Jeremy Mogford, a third generation restaurateur and hotelier, and converted to a hotel. Today it is an ideal place to relax or hide away. Little wonder Julia Stevens and Brenda Brooks use it for a secret lunch in *The Daughters of Cain*. Even Morse, in the same book, found himself falling ever so slightly in love with the reformed punk Ellie Smith – at least enough to treat her to a half bottle of Premier Cru champagne.

Morse knew and cared very little about money. The £18 he spent on champagne was only an extravagance when he compared it to the number of pints he could have bought for the same money, or realised it would have gone a good way towards a rare bottle of Glen Duich malt whisky.

He belonged to that middle-class pigeonhole his parents, had they remained together, would have labelled 'comfortable'. In 1969, soon after his transfer to CID, he took out a twenty-year mortgage on his North Oxford flat. By the mid-seventies, his promotion to Chief Inspector allowed him to invest a little more and he was persuaded by a likeable financial adviser from the Prudential to contribute £55 a month to a fifteen-year endowment policy. To celebrate his sixtieth birthday, the insurance company honoured its promise and the same salesman delivered a cheque for £12,000 plus profits – 'compared to the vast majority of mankind he was extremely fortunate'.

Petty about day-to-day finances, Morse saw no obvious advantage to his steadily increasing bank balance. He enjoyed few luxuries, other than music and books and whisky. His infrequent extravagances were not so much acts of spontaneous kindness as attempts to salve his mean-spiritedness. In *Morse's Greatest Mystery*, he enjoys the unaccustomed buzz of cheeriness when he uses his own money to replace £400 stolen from a pub's children's charity fund.

'Morse's meanness with money is inexcusable,' Colin Dexter readily admits. 'He is happy to allow Sergeant Lewis, on half the salary, to buy nine-tenths of his regular and excessive intake of alcohol.'

In *The Daughters of Cain*, Morse and Lewis return to Oxford after questioning the mother of a suicide victim. Turning left at the Martyrs' Memorial, Lewis parks his boss's Jaguar at the far end of Broad Street. 'Don't worry, Lewis,' Morse says. 'All the traffic wardens know my car. They'll think I'm on duty.'

'Which you are, Sir.'

'Which I am.'

Lewis follows his Chief Inspector into New College Lane and under the Bridge of Sighs and then left into the maze of back lanes and alleys beneath the walls of New College. Twenty or thirty more yards and the pair are outside the Turf Tavern. A notice above the entrance advises all patrons (although Morse is not a particularly tall man) to mind their heads (duck or grouse) and inside the rough-stoned, black-beamed rooms, the true connoisseur of beers can

seat himself at one of the small wooden tables and enjoy a finely cask-conditioned pint; and it is in order to drink and to talk and to think that patrons frequent this elusively situated tavern in a blessedly music – Muzak – free environment. It was time to talk over the brutal murder of Felix McClure and, as Lewis knew only too well, that meant a pint (several pints) for Morse and an orange juice for himself.

Arguably Oxford's oldest public house, the Turf Tavern is surrounded by venerable college buildings and built into part of the old city wall. Inside, its cramped, low-beamed bars make it a tourist attraction in its own right. This is Dickensian old England at its well-preserved finest.

Foundations beneath the Turf date from the thirteenth century. Like so much of Oxford, the site and building are owned by a university college, in this case Merton. The surviving timber frontage is four centuries older and was probably added when the building was a malthouse. By 1775, it was trading as a cider house and finally, around 1790, it became the Spotted Cow inn.

Although much of the original fabric has gone, the brewery has attempted to restore and fix the premises in an 1805 time-warp – the year it became the Turf Tavern. In fact, the interior is so atmospheric it is not surprising it was used in two television episodes – *The Silent World of Nicholas Quinn* and *Service of All the Dead*.

Whatever the mechanism of his inspiration, Morse does occasionally visit a public house for more than a drink. In *Death is Now My Neighbour*, he calls on Steven and Sonya Lowbridge, the landlords of Oxford's historic Bear Inn, hoping to pin down a snippet of evidence.

From its colourful sign overhanging the corner of Alfred Street and Blue Boar Street, the Bear Inn would seem to have more to do with the once popular but barbaric sport of bear baiting than its history as Oxford's premier coaching inn. One title it does win is that of being the city's smallest pub. It was not always so.

The existing Bear Inn dates back only as far as 1801. It inherited the name on the closure of much larger premises next door. That site was first occupied by Parne Hall until that building's destruction by fire in 1421. Rebuilt and renamed Le Tabard, its final name change came in 1432 when the Bear Inn makes its first appearance on city records.

Over the next hundred years, it grew to become one of the biggest taverns in Oxford. While circuit judges and royal commissions used its back rooms for regular hearings and meetings, the subjects of their jurisprudence drank and plotted various misdemeanours downstairs. And when the day's business was over, the Bear's bedrooms offered other distractions.

Fights and drunken brawls were common. Sometimes even the Law Lords found themselves a target. A gang of angry university scholars, protesting at the imprisonment of some Magdalen men accused of receiving poached deer from Shotover Royal Forest, besieged the Bear in 1586, eventually smashing their way in and ransacking a suite occupied by Lord Norris.

During the eighteenth century, the Bear established its reputation as the city's biggest and busiest coaching terminal. The legendary 'Oxford Machine' coach – the Concorde of its day – was based here until the Bear finally closed in 1801.

The name was immediately adopted by the sharp-witted publican of a smaller tavern next door, the Jolly Trooper, and it is into this pub, originally built as an ostler's house in 1606, that Morse stepped for the first time since his university days.

It was during Morse's final year at Oxford that the landlord, Alan Course, initiated what was to become a tradition.

> The Bear Inn was nationally – internationally – renowned for its ties: about 5,000 of them at the last count. Showcases of ties covered the walls, covered the ceilings, in each of the bars: ties from Army regiments, sports clubs, schools and OB associations; ties anywhere and everywhere. The collection started (Morse learned) in 1954, when the incumbent landlord had invited any customer with an interesting-looking tie to have the last three or four inches of its back-end cut off – in exchange for a couple of pints of beer. Thereafter, the snipped-off portions were put on display in cabinets, with a small square of white card affixed to each giving provenance and description.

In Death is Now My Neighbour *Morse visited the Bear Inn*
hoping to find a clue within its impressive tie collection

Armed with a photograph of a man wearing a maroon tie with a narrow white strip, Morse hoped what is claimed to be Britain's biggest tie collection would be able to pin down his suspect...or at least the school he had once attended...or the club he played football for. 'It's a bit like a farmer looking for a lost contact lens in a ploughed field,' he confessed to Steven Lowbridge.

Morse drew a blank and gave up squinting at the endless bits of somebody's tie. When the publican's wife returned he showed her the picture. 'That what you're looking for?' asked Sonya Lowbridge, pointing at the inch or two of knotted tie visible in the photograph.

'That's it,' nodded the policeman.

'I can tell you where you can find that.'

Morse's eyes widened. 'You can?'

'Yep,' said Sonya. 'You'll find one just like that in the tie-rack at Marks and Spencer.'

Sadly, some of Morse's favourite public houses have not survived, at least not as he would want to remember them. Morse once drank quite regularly at The Mitre, a little way down the High Street. Not any more, at least not since its new owners converted it to a restaurant. Beer, he regularly informed Lewis, was 'pure food'. It didn't need adulterating with the real stuff.

In his 1795 edition of *Travels in England*, the German clergyman Pastor Moritz describes how he was taken by a companion to The Mitre tavern and found it full of inebriated parsons enthusiastically debating passages from the Bible. Margaret Bowman, in search of a different kind of spirit, drinks two double scotches at The Mitre in *The Secret of Annexe 3* before continuing down the High Street to the Church of St Mary the Virgin.

Although it claims to have been serving alcohol to the public since 1261, the present Mitre Inn dates from around 1630. The site has always belonged to Lincoln College and the name probably derives from the college's coat of arms, which depicts the mitre of the Bishop of Lincoln. But it was as a coaching inn that The Mitre earned its reputation.

Services began as early as 1671 when a London coach left Oxford three times a week. Between 1790 and 1798, the *Universal Business Directory* contained the following entry:

> From the Mitre Inn, High-street:- Messrs. Slater and Gray's heavy-coach sets
> out every morning, at seven o'clock, through Henly, to the Bell Savage,
> Ludgate-hill, London, Sunday excepted; inside fare 14s., outside 8s. W.W.
> Sydenham, proprietor, at Oxford.

The Mitre's status as a coaching inn appears to have increased with the arrival of the railways. With the closure of its main rival, the Angel Hotel, its 1852 schedule lists services to six destinations including London, Birmingham, Cheltenham and Worcester. Sadly, the last evidence of The Mitre's coaching heritage was destroyed in 1926 when the adjoining Turl Street stables were converted into the Turl Bar. Now a Grade II listed building, The Mitre's former bedrooms were 'repossessed' in 1969 to provide accommodation for students.

Other premises have survived only a little longer than Morse himself. At the conclusion of *Service of All the Dead*, he takes Lewis to The Friar Bacon at Elsfield, just north of the A40 ring road, to explain the 'extremely odd points' in the case. The sign outside portraying the great thirteenth-century scientist and philosopher as a stout, jolly-looking Franciscan monk was obviously once as pleasing to Morse as the Morrell's Oxford Bitter inside. The pub was demolished in May 2000.

Each year, thousands of Morse fans descend on Oxford intent on discovering more about one of the world's favourite fictional detectives. Armed with notes and maps and cameras

In The Secret of Annexe 3 *Margaret Bowman visits
The Mitre – something Morse stopped doing long before*

they enthusiastically follow in Morse's footsteps, attempting to experience or unearth just a little more about his life. One mystery – never quite solved in the novels – is the exact location of Morse's North Oxford bachelor flat.

From the opening pages of *The Secret of Annexe 3*, we know that Morse lives within a few minutes' drive of the Old Parsonage Hotel – not far, in fact, from where Colin Dexter has his own home. But there, among the grand old Victorian houses, the trail goes cold.

So what *do* we know? Only that by the late 1960s, the majority of houses in the streets straddling the Banbury Road, and built originally to house the families of university dons, had been converted and divided into three or four self-contained flats. We know Morse's flat is in a 'tiny cul-de-sac' and we know it is called Leys Close – at least, in Colin Dexter's imagination.

A few years further on, we know Morse lived in the same flat until his death and we are informed of the exact address – 45 The Flats, Banbury Road, Oxford. For a more accurate, but still inconclusive, location we must turn to *The Remorseful Day* and the site of Morse's local.

Not long into what would be Morse's final investigation, he leaves his flat to visit one of his favourite pubs with its flower-filled window boxes and superb view of St Edwards School cricket ground.

> He walked down South Parade to the Woodstock Road, turned right, and soon found himself at the Woodstock Arms, where the landlady rightly prided herself on a particularly fine pint of Morrell's Bitter – of which Morse took liberal advantage. The printed menu and the chalked-up specials on the board were strong temptations to many a man. But not to Morse. These past two decades he had almost invariably taken his lunchtime calories in liquid form; and he did so now.

Godstow Nunnery where Henry II installed his mistress Rosamund the Fair

Escaping from his office on the first floor of the Thames Valley Police headquarters at Kidlington, Morse's favoured 'thinking' pub is situated a little way down the A34 at Lower Wolvercote. The Trout Inn was a pub he often visited alone. Sitting at a table on the paved terrace between the pub wall and the river parapet, he slowly and methodically went over *The Way Through the Woods* inquiry.

The Trout and its surroundings are probably the most famous and photogenic of any Morse location. The seventeenth-century inn and nearby Wolvercote village also play crucial parts in *The Jewel That Was Ours*. The history of the Trout Inn, which has associations with both Matthew Arnold and Lewis Carroll, is equally fascinating – and frightening.

Godstow Nunnery, which lies on the opposite bank of the river on Trout Island, was built in 1133 and consecrated in 1179 by the Archbishop of Canterbury in the presence of

Henry II. It will forever be linked with Rosamund the Fair, the tragic heroine of possibly the most romantic of English legends.

Rosamund was the daughter of Walter de Clifford and the much-loved mistress of Henry II. Tradition has it that he kept her sheltered in a secret garden, defended by his knight Sir Thomas, and protected by a labyrinth which could only be safely entered by following a silver thread. In 1175, Henry left to go to war. Rosamund's pleas to be allowed to travel with the royal party were refused. While the king was away, Queen Eleanor, furious with jealousy, killed Sir Thomas and stole the silver thread. She made her way through the maze and forced Rosamund to drink from a poisoned chalice.

In another version of Rosamund's death, Henry would occasionally return and stay at the Trout Inn. To signal his presence, the king would place a lantern in his bedroom window and his lover, seeing the light, would make her way through a secret tunnel beneath the river to join him. One night, while the king was still away, Queen Eleanor tricked her rival by placing a lantern in the same window. As Rosamund emerged from the tunnel the queen stabbed her with a dagger.

Rosamund the Fair – whose existence has long been accepted by historians – still returns to the Trout Inn. Known locally as the White Lady, she pays regular visits to the Trout, as staff and scores of customers will testify. Rosamund's ghost walks on the original floor of the Trout – extra flagstones taken from the ruins of Godstow Nunnery have been added – but it is visible only from the knees upwards.

In May 2000, a member of the Trout's staff reported seeing the White Lady, accompanied by a sudden and chilling temperature drop.

'I was putting the chairs on the tables,' she recalled, 'and as I looked down the building, I saw a figure move slowly across a doorway. I assumed it was one of my colleagues and thought nothing of it. When I returned to the main part of the pub, I discovered no one had been near my area for at least twenty minutes.'

Rosamund has also been known to knock bottles off tables and appear behind the bar, which was once a bedroom, while the Trout is open and full of customers. Corners of the pub, which does not have air conditioning, have plunged to freezing while crowded with summer visitors. But the commonest manifestation reported by customers is a sudden and unexplained smell of heather – Rosamund was buried with a sprig of heather placed in her tomb.

Piety and scandal permeated Godstow Nunnery in equal measure. During Rosamund's six-year affair with Henry II, she bore him two sons. And for several centuries, the Benedictine nuns were notorious for providing 'hospitality' to Oxford's novice monks.

During the dissolution of the monasteries in the 1540s, Henry VIII had most of the buildings demolished. Those that were left were turned into homes. Material from the derelict monastery was transported across the river and used to build a fisherman's house. By 1625, the building had been enlarged and, as Godstow House, was trading as an inn.

During the Civil War siege of Oxford, Godstow became the site of a bitter and destructive skirmish between Roundheads and Royalists. A troop of Parliamentarian cavalry was despatched from Banbury to arrest a 'gentleman of quality' who had taken refuge in Godstow House. His Royalist supporters first fortified and defended the remains of Godstow Nunnery and then, forced to retreat, defended Godstow Bridge. When the Roundheads finally broke through, the fugitive – thought to be David Walter – escaped from Godstow House and the building was set ablaze by his pursuers.

By 1720, Godstow House had been rebuilt, again using masonry from the nunnery, and was trading as the Trout Inn. Stables added in 1737 are still visible today.

A short walk away is Wolvercote Green and the Plough Inn with its magnificent winter views of the sun setting over the Wytham Hills. Recovering in hospital from a perforated ulcer, Morse reads *Murder on the Oxford Canal* and becomes obsessed with solving the 1859 murder of Joanna Franks. Dragged from the nearby Oxford Canal, the woman's body was taken to the Plough Inn where it was examined by a police surgeon.

Beyond the Wolvercote and further up the Godstow Road, a journey Morse and Lewis make several times in *The Way Through the Woods*, is the White Hart at Wytham. The only building in the village not to be owned by Oxford University, it was built in the fifteenth century and takes it name from an albino deer called the White Hart. This rare deer was thought to bring good fortune to those who saw it and extreme bad luck to anyone who harmed it.

Invited back to the White Hart by the pathologist Max de Bryn after the discovery of a body in Wytham Woods, Morse declines the offer of a drink, saying he must return for an urgent Kidlington meeting. A few days later, he returns with Lewis to try a pint of 'whatever the locals drink'.

Morse is a man burdened with an almost crippling set of phobias – nyctophobia, a childish fear of the dark; arachnophobia, a dread of spiders; aerophobia, a terror of flying; and hypsophobia, the panic triggered by any exposed height. Since his earliest years as a policeman, another complex fear had gripped Morse. Yet he was not, as everyone thought, afraid of the sight of dead bodies:

> What he really suffered from was a completely new phobia, one that was all his own: the fear of being sick at the sight of bodies which had met their deaths in strange or terrible circumstances. Even Morse, for all his classical education, was unable to coin an appropriately descriptive, or etymologically accurate, term for such a phobia: and even had he been so able, the word would certainly have been pretentiously polysyllabic.

In July 1982, Morse receives a telephone call from Sergeant Lewis. 'We've got a body, Sir – or at least part...' Reluctantly, the Chief Inspector leaves his office (and less reluctantly the pile of paperwork) and collects his car from the police headquarters yard.

> Two miles north of police headquarters in Kidlington, on the main A423 road to Banbury, an elbow turn to the right leads, after only three hundred yards or so, to the Boat Inn, which, together with about twenty cottages, a farm, and a depot of the Inland Waterways Executive, comprises the tiny hamlet of Thrupp. The inn itself, only some thirty yards from the waters of the Oxford Canal, has served generations of boatmen, past and present. But the working barges of earlier times, which brought down coal from the Midlands and shipped up beer from the Oxford breweries, have now yielded place to the privately owned long-boats and pleasure-cruisers which ply their way placidly along the present waterway.

Confronted by the sight of a head-less and limb-less corpse, Morse is in need of a drink. Accompanied by Lewis and Max the pathologist, he persuades the landlord of the Boat Inn to side-step the licensing laws by furnishing the trio with a private back room and an out-of-hours bottle of Glenfiddich. When *The Riddle of the Third Mile* was adapted for television as *The Last Enemy*, it is Dr Grayling Russell who arrives to examine the corpse after Max de Bryn's fatal heart attack. It is Lewis, however, drinking alone in the Boat Inn while his superior is away in London, who discovers that one of the *Riddle*'s 'missing' suspects, Lonsdale geography don George Westerby, owns a canalside cottage as an angling retreat – and the murder mystery begins to unravel.

More than a decade later, Morse and Lewis return to the Boat Inn, this time to talk over the apparently motiveless murder of the physiotherapist Rachel James in *Death Is Now My Neighbour*. After a couple of beers, they try to solve the riddle of a seventeenth-century verse typed on the back of a postcard found at the crime scene.

Long before Morse discovered the Boat Inn at Thrupp, midway between Kidlington and Shipton-on-Cherwell, the hostelry was in turn a necessity and then a pleasure for those who first worked and then relaxed on the Oxford Canal. Today, only the inn and a row of picturesque canal bank terraced cottages attract the visitors. But Thrupp existed long before the construction of the waterway. It was first recorded in the *Domesday Book* as Trop, the Old English for hamlet or farm, and rented to Wadard by its owner Roger d'Ivry. Wadard was an heroic and noted officer in the Norman army and is seen on the Bayeux tapestry organising supplies.

Returning to Oxford, there is one place that features not only throughout Morse's life, both as a student and a police officer, but also as a backdrop in the majority of Colin Dexter's novels. The Randolph is the city's most prestigious and elegant hotel – it would also appear to have an unusually high mortality rate among its guests.

Less than an hour after the arrival of a group of American tourists, Laura Stratton dies from an apparent heart attack in room 310. Far more sinister, at least for Morse, is the disappearance of her handbag containing the Wolvercote Tongue, a jewelled artefact unearthed by the dead woman's first husband, which she intended donating, during her brief Oxford visit, to the Ashmolean Museum.

In the short story *Last Call*, Peter Sherwood is found dead in room 231. The pathologist assigned to the case is convinced the diabetic businessman suffered a massive heart attack and collapsed in his room just minutes after arriving for a conference – but Morse is not so sure.

By some quirk of fate, it is on the same landing, this time in room 210, that Frank Harrison, whose wife's murder triggers *The Remorseful Day* investigation, spends the weekend with a 'sultrily attractive' woman in her late twenties.

The Randolph's location – and its place amid the architecture of Oxford – is best appreciated from its Spires Restaurant. Here, surrounded by a full collection of college crests, you can look out from the two north-facing windows over:

> … Beaumont Street, with the Ashmolean Museum and the
> Taylorian Institute just across the way; whilst those seated beside the
> three equally large windows on the eastern side look out on to the
> Martyrs' Memorial with St John's and Balliol Colleges beyond it,
> sharing with their fellow diners a vista of St Giles', the widest street
> in Oxford and visually one of the most attractive avenues in
> England.

Contrary to popular belief, the Randolph was not named after Randolph Churchill, but took its name from the now disappeared Randolph Gallery, which in turn was named after the Ashmolean benefactor and Principal of St Albans Hall, the Reverend Dr Francis Randolph. Another notable eighteenth-century member of the family was Dr John Randolph, who held four professorships and three bishoprics in turn and was famous for his interminable candle-lit lectures delivered to slumbering students.

Work started on the hotel's Beaumont Street site in 1864 after months of bitter debate. John Ruskin was in favour of a plan submitted by Sir George Gilbert Smith, which advocated a Gothic revival. The city council, which did not want to see a neo-Gothic style extended into Georgian Beaumont Street, disagreed. A compromise was eventually agreed and a design by William Wilkinson, described as 'Scottish Early English' and similar to the University Museum, was approved.

Opened on 17 February 1866, the newspapers and periodicals lost no time in extolling the virtues of this 'first class hotel for families and gentlemen':

> Entering by the portico in Beaumont Street, the visitor notices the
> mosaic flooring of the hall, the conservatory in the rear, and a
> massive staircase of Portland stone, leading to the various landings
> and corridors. The railing is of iron, with ornamental pillars and
> timber coping, the stairs being of a width recalling the baronial
> mansions of older time, and doubly carpeted.

Morse was less concerned with the gothic architecture of the Randolph Hotel
than the fact that its bar 'serves a decent pint'

By 1910, various improvements had been made and a hotel brochure claimed the Randolph not only offered the benefits of 'electric lighting throughout' and an 'American elevator' but 'many handsome suites of rooms with very charming prospects'. Today, the yellow-brick building contains more artistic treasures. The Lancaster Room and Spires Restaurant both contain paintings by Sir Osbert Lancaster, commissioned to illustrate Max Beerbohm's satire on Oxford life, *Zuleika Dobson*.

The hotel is as much a favourite with Morse as it is with most visitors to Oxford. It was here that Wendy Spencer had worked as a waitress in the dying weeks of their affair. But it is the hotel's Chapter Bar that Morse regularly favours – 'If there's a bar anywhere in Britain with a better view than this...' – and where the seeds of doubt are sown as he read the newspaper cutting detailing the St Frideswide's deaths in *Service of All the Dead*. And it is to this bar that he and Lewis retreat to discuss the discovery of Paddy Flynn's body on a council waste tip in *The Remorseful Day*.

It is not surprising that the Randolph appears as an impressive location in the television dramas. Several scenes in *The Wolvercote Tongue* – which became *The Jewel That Was Ours* – were filmed in the hotel, including the medieval dinner. Insisting on his Hitchcock-style cameo in each of the television films, Colin Dexter can be glimpsed supping a pint as Morse and Lewis enjoy a drink in the Chapter Bar. Other adaptations in which the Randolph features are *Service of All the Dead* and *Second Time Around*.

Sipping coffee in the Lancaster Room at the Randolph, Morse and Lewis mull over the disappearance of the Wolvercote Jewel and the two deaths:

> 'We're getting plenty of suspects, Sir.'
> 'Mm. We're getting pretty high on content but very low on
> analysis, wouldn't you say? I'll be all right once the bar opens.'
> 'It is open – opened half-past ten.'
> 'Why are we drinking *this* stuff, then?'

How many killers and their victims have climbed the Randolph Hotel's impressive staircase?

Old Oxford
and New Murders

God gave us memory so that we may have
June roses in the middle of winter.

AUTHOR UNKNOWN

IN 1856, THE AMERICAN writer Nathaniel Hawthorne arrived in Oxford. On the whole he enjoyed his stay but one thing that caught his attention so intrigued him, he thought it worth noting in his diary. It was the quality of the stone.

Dwarfed by the splendour of the buildings and the upright dignity of the University, the antiquity of the city's stonework may seem to be unimportant, but not for Hawthorne. 'It is,' he reported in his *English Note-Book*, 'a stone found in the neighbourhood of Oxford, and very soon begins to crumble and decay superficially...so that twenty years do the work of a hundred.'

For those who enjoy such things, the allegory is not wasted on Morse. Although a tiny splinter in the fabric of Oxford, Morse's own condition turns out to be as 'fragile and powdery' as that attacked by Hawthorne's walking stick.

Never worth a mention in the first four or five novels, although he has an injured foot in *Last Bus to Woodstock*, the Chief Inspector's health appears to become almost a sub-plot in the later books and television episodes. At first he has a niggling toothache, in *The Riddle of the Third Mile* and *The Last Enemy*, and in *The Wench is Dead*, a perforated ulcer and an emergency hospital admission become the very fulcrum on which the mystery turns.

Three books later, in *The Daughters of Cain*, he is back in hospital with dangerously high blood pressure and an off-the-scale cholesterol level. Diagnosed, treated and comfortable in his hospital bed, Morse makes the most of his situation.

As he lay back after the sister had gone, and switched on the headphones to
Classic FM, Morse was again aware of how low he had sunk, since almost
everything – a kindly look, a kindly word, a kindly thought, even the thought
of a kindly thought – seemed to push him ever nearer to the rim of tears.
Forget it, Morse! Forget your health! For a while anyway. He picked up The
ABC Murders which he'd found in the meagre ward library. He'd always
enjoyed Agatha Christie: a big fat puzzle ready for the reader from page one.

The lesson, if indeed there was one for Morse, was forgotten as quickly as the depression of
inactivity. Allowed home in *Death is Now My Neighbour* after emergency treatment for
diabetes, Morse made straight for the nearest pub. Downing a pint of Bass he explained to
a dubious Lewis how it was possible to balance his insulin-sugar intake with almost any
food – including beer.

The promises and resolutions to stop smoking and start exercising were soon forgotten
and we read the final books as if following the decline of a 'dear old friend'.

Colin Dexter's own health, although thankfully never as neglected as his hero's, has
proved inspirational for more than one Morse book and television story line. He is diabetic
and has certainly seen the inside of one or two hospitals. 'But I get quite a few ideas from
being deaf because I mishear so much,' he explains.

The Silent World of Nicholas Quinn is dedicated to Jack Ashley, the campaigning deaf
former Member of Parliament. A character in the book makes a fatal lip-reading mistake.
'I knew what was going to happen from the very nature of the book,' says Dexter. 'The
sleight of hand begins immediately and Morse goes for one name instead of the other.'

Inspiration for his other novels comes from a variety of sources, as we shall see. But to
unravel *The Wench is Dead*, we must return to Morse's first near-fatal illness. It all started
on a Saturday morning in November 1989. Morse's part-time cleaning lady, Mrs Green,
arrived to find her employer slumped against his hall wall, the front of his deckchair-striped
pyjamas stained with curiously unmixed dribbles of blood and vomit. By 10.30 a.m. Morse
had been delivered by ambulance to the Accident and Emergency Department of the John
Radcliffe Hospital where a doctor confidently announced Morse was suff ng from a
perforated ulcer.

At that point Morse knew that the Angel of Death had fluttered its wing above his head; and
he felt a sudden frisson of fear, as for the first time in his life he began to think of dying. For
in his mind's eye, though just for a second or two, he thought he almost caught sight of the
laudatory obituary, the creditable paragraph.

When Lewis arrived to see him the following evening, his superior was feeling moderately
better and already looking for some kind of distraction. It came, at least momentarily, in the

form of a bottle of lemon-and-barley (immediately confiscated) and a small bottle of Bell's whisky (immediately concealed). Lewis's plastic carrier also contained two books: *Scales of Injustice: A Comparative Study of Crime and its Punishment as Recorded in the County of Shropshire, 1842–1852* (a gift from Mrs Lewis), and the gently titillating *The Blue Ticket* (a gift from Sergeant Lewis).

An hour after Lewis's departure, Morse received a third volume, this time delivered by the widow of a patient whose death on the ward he had hazily witnessed earlier that morning.

Murder on the Oxford Canal, researched and written by Wilfrid M. Deniston and printed privately under the auspices of The Oxford and County Local History Society, described the rape and murder of a middle-aged woman more than a century earlier. Morse read the twenty-odd pages with growing interest. However bad the pain of his ulcer or the indignity of his hospital stay, Morse had found the very thing he needed to help him survive:

> The theoretical problem which his mind had suddenly seized upon was no
> more than a bit of harmless, quite inconsequential amusement. And yet the
> doubts persisted in his brain: could anyone, *anyone*, read this story and not find
> himself questioning one or two of the points so confidently reported? Or two or
> three of them? Or three or four?

Morse re-read the first section of the late historian's book. The murder victim is Joanna Franks, a dressmaker and designers' model, whose body is found early on 22 June 1859, floating in the triangular-shaped basin of the Oxford Canal about two-and-a-half miles north of the (then) city-centre canal terminus at Hayfield Wharf.

Franks was on her way to London to join her ostler husband. The four-man crew of the canal boat *Barbary Bray* were later arrested and three stood trial at Oxford Summer Assizes charged with 'wilful murder, by casting, pushing, and throwing the said Joanna Franks into the Oxford Canal by which means she was choked, suffocated, and drowned'. The jury was directed to return a not-guilty verdict on a charge of rape.

According to Deniston's account, two of the crew, Jack Oldfield and Alfred Musson, claimed their co-accused Walter Towns took a less active part in the night's drama. The court agreed. Oldfield and Musson were publicly hanged at Oxford while Towns was transported to Australia for life.

As ever, Morse is not convinced. 'If the crewmen had not been responsible, who on earth had?' Confined, at least for the foreseeable future, to his hospital bed, he persuaded Sergeant Lewis and the daughter of a fellow patient to undertake the detective legwork.

The roots of *The Wench is Dead*, Colin Dexter's eighth Morse novel and the winner of a Crime Writers' Association Gold Dagger, can be traced to a best-selling 1950s' crime thriller,

and its inspiration to a real nineteenth-century murder – and twentieth-century 'haunting'.

In the 1951 novel *The Daughter of Time*, Josephine Tey's hospital-bound Scotland Yard detective enlists the help of an historical researcher to solve the mystery of who really killed the young Princes in the Tower, the true heirs to the Crown of England. Together they sort through the layers of dynastic propaganda, follow the threads woven by cloistered chroniclers and examine actual texts and documents and letters. Josephine Tey was a pseudonym under which the Scottish author and playwright Elizabeth Mackintosh published mystery novels. *The Daughter of Time* was an immediate success and it was reprinted twenty times.

The actual canal murder on which *The Wench is Dead* is based took place twenty years before the crime and wrongful convictions Morse was about to unravel. Early in June 1839, Christina Collins – Joanna Franks in the Dexter novel – received a letter from her husband Robert urging her to join him in London. The cheapest way to make the journey from Liverpool to the capital was by barge and on 15 June she took a canal boat to begin her journey south.

The next day she arrived at Preston Brook, just east of Runcorn, purchased a through ticket from the Pickford & Company office and boarded one of its express boats. There were four crew members – James Owen, the thirty-nine-year-old captain; George Thomas; William Ellis; and a teenaged deckhand called

opposite and over: The Oxford canal runs for 77 miles from Hawksbury Junction near Coventry to Oxford where it joins the Thames

William Musson. The journey began quietly, but the crew progressively became drunk and abusive and violent.

Collins, by all accounts a petite and well-educated young woman, no longer felt safe sitting alone in the long boat's cabin. Threatened by the men's crude and cruel sexual imputations, she insisted on walking along the towpath. Each time she returned to the boat she was berated for her prudity. When it became too dark to follow the barge's progress on foot, she once again retreated to the cabin.

Exactly what happened during the night will never be known. The three older members of the crew each played a part in beating and raping and finally murdering their passenger. Musson, all three repeatedly claimed, had innocently slept through the attacks.

By dawn the next morning, 17 June, the vessel had passed Brindley Bank on the Trent and Mersey Canal. A boatman noticed something floating in the canal and used a boat hook to pull it to the side. Collins may well have been alive; her body was still warm and as she was carried up a flight of sandstone steps beside Rugeley Aqueduct, blood still dripped from her wounds.

The crew of the Pickford flyboat were arrested further down the cut although William Musson was soon released. But as evidence of the trio's gruesome crime was being laid before Stafford Assizes, a second bizarre tale was finding its own place in local legend.

Despite several attempts to scrub clean the steps up which Christina Collins' body had been carried, the bloodstains always returned. For decades, scores of witnesses claim to have witnessed the phenomenon of the 'Bloody Steps' while others, including a police constable and a local vicar, reported seeing the ghostly figure of a young woman on the towpath. The enigmatic flow of blood ceased when the original pre-Victorian steps were replaced with a concrete flight.

The adult boatmen were all found guilty of Collins' murder. Owen and Thomas were hanged and their bodies buried in Stafford jail. Ellis was sentenced to transportation for life. His punishment was later reduced to fourteen years, but he never returned from Australia.

The Oxford Canal features, although far less dominantly, in a second Morse novel. In *The Dead of Jericho* – the first Morse story to be adapted for television – mention of the waterway drifts in and out of the text like a benign but ever-present mist.

Morse had lost count of how many times he had toured the local hostelries as a student. In the early 1950s there seemed to be a pub on every corner. One, in Jericho's Walton Street, is almost certainly responsible for giving the area its name.

The Oxford Canal: a real 1839 canal murder provided
the inspiration for The Wench is Dead

In the middle years of the seventeenth century, a tavern was built north west of Oxford. The inn was within Walton Manor, whose grand house stood where St Sepulchre's Cemetery now lies, and was surrounded by the fertile and productive Jericho Gardens and allotments. It was natural, according to local legend, that the hostelry should take the name of the Jericho Tavern.

Another traditional tale has a more biblical pedigree. Taken from the parable of the Good Samaritan, Jericho signifies a traveller's refuge. Arriving after sunset by one of the two ancient tracks that crossed Port Meadow to find the Oxford city gates already closed, Jericho Tavern was a convenient overnight lodgings. In fact, it was the only place to stay until the gates opened at dawn the next morning.

Colin Dexter offers his theory in the opening pages of *The Dead of Jericho*:

> Here, in the criss-cross grid of streets with names like 'Wellington' and 'Nelson' and the other mighty heroes, are the dwellings built for those who worked on the wharves or on the railway, at the University Press or at Lucy's iron foundry in Juxon Street. But the visitor to the City Museum in St Aldate's will find no *Guide to Jericho* along the shelves; and even by the oldest of its own inhabitants, the provenance of that charming and mysterious name of 'Jericho' is variously – and dubiously – traced. Some claim that in the early days…the whistle of a passing train from the lines across the canal could make the walls come tumbling down; others would point darkly to the synagogue in Richmond Road and talk of sharp and profitable dealings in the former Jewish quarter; yet others lift their eyes to read the legend on a local inn: 'Tarry ye at Jericho until your beards be grown.'

One fact is undisputed – the area remained of little importance until the construction of the Oxford Canal.

Up to the last quarter of the eighteenth century, every nugget of coal used to fire the city's factories and warm its homes was colliered from the north-east pits to the south of England and then transported up from London. By 1769, the demand for coal was so great, a quicker and cheaper method of supply needed to be found, and work started on a canal to link Oxford with the coalfields of Warwickshire.

The cost of the Oxford Canal was £307,000. It was financed by a consortium of city bodies and dignitaries including Oxford University, the City Corporation, the Duke of Marlborough and the then Prime Minister, Lord North.

St Barnabas' Church and the Oxford Canal provide
the backdrop for The Dead of Jericho

Horse-drawn longboats making the ninety-one-mile journey from Hawkesbury, near Coventry, to Oxford's New Road terminal had to negotiate twenty-eight locks, forty-one wagon bridges and thirty-eight wooden lift bridges. The new coal artery was so successful that the Duke of Marlborough immediately began work on a branch to Wolvercote –

The one-time slums of Jericho are now sought-after city residences

Duke's Cut – to supply fuel to the villages of the upper Thames.

Thousands of navvies and itinerant craftsmen descended on Jericho and by the time the city link with the Trent and Mersey rivers was completed in 1790, Oxford possessed its first ghetto.

Other, more permanent, industries soon followed. In 1825, the Jericho Iron and Brass Foundry opened. A year later, work started on the new Oxford University Press building. The demand for cheap local housing was growing and the land opposite the Radcliffe Infirmary, which opened in 1770, was laid out in progressively built grids of streets: the canal to the west, Walton Street to the east, Worcester College to the south, and St Sepulchre's Cemetery bordering the north.

The houses were tight and cramped and lacked even the most basic sanitation, and were financed almost exclusively by greedy and speculative colleges such as St John's and Lucy's. Drinking water had to be collected in buckets, and the air, polluted by nearby foundries and dampened by the canal, was heavy and noxious.

Stinginess did not restrict itself to the university landlords. As the sloping ground towards the canal – and beyond to the River Isis – was progressively drained, the streets were developed. With the completion of Canal Street in 1870, Thomas Coombe, the superintendent of the Clarendon Press, identified an urgent need for some form of ecclesiastical guidance and agreed to finance the building of Jericho's first parish church. Discussing the plans for St Barnabas' Church, the pre-Raphaelite patron ordered his architect 'not to throw a penny away on external appearance and decoration'.

Spiritual guidance and ample employment were not enough. By the second half of Queen Victoria's reign, the back-to-back terraces had degenerated into soulless slums and three cholera epidemics had already devastated its ill-fed population.

It is in the desperate streets of Jericho – renamed Beersheba in the parish of St Silas – that Jude Fawley, a Wessex villager of intellect and promise, arrives to study at Christminster (Oxford) in Thomas Hardy's 1895 novel *Jude the Obscure*. At first encouraged and then betrayed by his schoolmaster, Phillotson, the young Fawley works as a stonemason while continuing his studies, hoping one day to be admitted to the University. Morse, who believed the human condition rarely changed, would have felt familiar, weaving his way through Hardy's plot of lies, deceit, masochism, unrequited love and fallen ambition.

By the time Morse arrives at Anne Scott's house in Canal Reach (Canal Street) in *The Dead of Jericho*, the area has changed almost beyond recognition. Many of the slums so familiar to Hardy have been demolished and the remaining two-up two-down homes restored and renovated. Jericho is now a desirable location for young professionals.

Thankfully for Morse, many of the original hostelries remain. The original Jericho Tavern on Walton Street was rebuilt in 1818 and a third storey added before it reopened as the Jericho House. In keeping with the area's new image, it is now called the Philanderer and Firkin.

Anne Scott and George Jackson – the dead of Jericho – live at the far end of Canal Reach, opposite the entrance of which stands the fictional Printer's Devil public house. It was in here that Morse downed a couple of stiff whiskies. His creator found the original further up Canal Street under the sign of the Bookbinder's Arms.

As a teenager, Morse had invested a few shillings in a book on architecture and spent the following weeks touring the churches and historic buildings of Lincolnshire, attempting to trace the time-line of the designs. In the end he gave up on the intricacies of Corinthian and Palladian and Baroque and confined the words – if not the architecture – to that part of his brain dedicated to solving crossword puzzles.

He was not a particular fan of museums, either. In *The Daughters of Cain*, his inquiries took him to a dominant and proud building opposite Keble College. Morse's lifelong fondness for trains whimsically suggested to him that the architecture might have been inspired by London's St Pancras railway station. Somewhere Morse had once read the history of the University Museum. It was, he recalled, the product of an 1849 Fellows meeting at which it was resolved to finance and construct a new building to bring together all the 'materials explanatory of the organic beings placed upon the globe'.

---

over: Inaugurated in 1849 the University Museum was built to bring together all 'the materials explanatory of the organic beings placed upon the globe'

Unlike the old humanities, which could be demonstrated in a lecture theatre, the rapidly expanding sciences needed laboratories, and a block of land to the east of Parks Road was earmarked for the project. But it was not until 20 June 1855 that the foundation stone was laid and a further five years before the museum, and the Inorganic Chemistry Laboratory alongside, were complete.

The design of the new museum soon proved as controversial as the opinions that filled its impressive interior. Several critics felt its Gothic style was 'detestable' and 'indecent', and should be reserved exclusively for religious structures.

To inaugurate the new venue, the British Oxford Association organised a debate between the Bishop of Oxford, Samuel Wilberforce, and Professor Thomas Huxley to discuss Darwin's theory of evolution. The meeting crackled with argument and counter-argument and the Bishop delivered what he thought would be a conclusive defence when he asked Huxley: 'Was it through your grandfather or grandmother that you allege your descent from a monkey?'

Huxley waited for the gasps of indignation to die away before answering: 'Sir, I am not ashamed to have a monkey for an ancestor, but I would be ashamed to be connected with a man who used great gifts to obscure the truth.'

A second shock wave rippled through the audience and one of the less robust female listeners fainted. The meeting eventually degenerated into a near riot and was abandoned.

Other, less well documented, controversies have woven themselves into the museum's history. The Dublin company chosen to build the museum hired two stonemason brothers to carve all the birds and animals incorporated into the window surrounds. Although talented craftsmen, the O'Shea brothers did have a fondness for drink and soon found themselves berated for their boisterous behaviour by watchful dons. It was several weeks before the university officials discovered their own features caricatured in stone. Unfortunately, all evidence of the O'Shea's mischievous revenge was ordered to be destroyed.

The tale brought a smile to Morse's face as he worked his way through the glass-roofed and galleried University Museum, between a statue of the Prince Consort and a stuffed ostrich, to enter the Pitt-Rivers Museum of Ethnology. While investigating *The Daughters of Cain*, Morse discovered that an exhibit from the Pitt-Rivers Museum had been used to murder two people, Dr Felix McClur and former Wolsey College scout Ted Brooks.

---

*The Pitt-Rivers Museum holds the key to
the murder in* The Daughters of Cain

One of the great ethnological collections of the world, the museum was specially designed and built to house the thousands of items amassed by Lieutenant-General Augustus Henry Lane Fox Pitt-Rivers. A career officer for more than fifty years, Pitt-Rivers served with the Grenadier Guards during the Crimean War before the War Office discovered his talent for experimental research and placed him in charge of a programme to improve the army's standard rifle. It was during this work that Pitt-Rivers began collecting firearms and then expanded his collection to include other weapons.

Since the specimens were moved to Oxford in the 1880s from their original home at the South Kensington Museum, the collection has continued to grow. It was fascinating, but not to Morse's taste:

> Morse spent a while wandering vaguely around the galleries. On the ground floor he gave as much of his attention as he could muster to the tall, glass show-cases illustrating the evolution of fire-arms, Japanese Noh masks, the history of Looms and Weaving, old musical instruments, shields, pots, models of boats, bull-roarers, North American dress, and myriad precious and semi-precious stones... Then, feeling like a man who in some great picture gallery has had his fill of fourteenth-century crucifixions, he walked up a flight of stone steps to see what the Upper Gallery had to offer; and duly experienced a similar sense of satiety as he ambled aimlessly along a series of black-wood, glass-topped display-cases, several containing scores of axes, aszes, tongs, scissors, keys, coins, animal-traps, specialized tools... Burmese, Siamese, Japanese, Indonesian...

It was a single exhibit in Oxford's perhaps most famous museum that gave Colin Dexter the idea for a story that was to become both a *Morse* television episode and later a novel. Dexter first suggested the story line for *The Wolvercote Tongue* – screened at Christmas 1987 – and then developed and published it as *The Jewel That Was Ours* three years later.

For those dedicated enough to trace the idea back to its source, a display cabinet in the Ashmolean Museum and a small Saxon relic hold the key.

Alfred the Great was one of the most inspirational kings ever to rule mankind. He defended Anglo-Saxon England from Viking raids, formulated a code of laws, and fostered the rebirth of religion and learning. He was also centuries ahead of his time by inventing the public-relations freebie.

One of Alfred's scholastic achievements was a translation of Gregory the Great's *Pastoral Care*, a copy of which he presented to each bishopric in his kingdom, and with each manuscript went a jewelled 'aestel' or reading pointer. These were not cheap gifts. Each pointer was worth fifty mancuses – gold coins – and consisted of an enamelled figure set

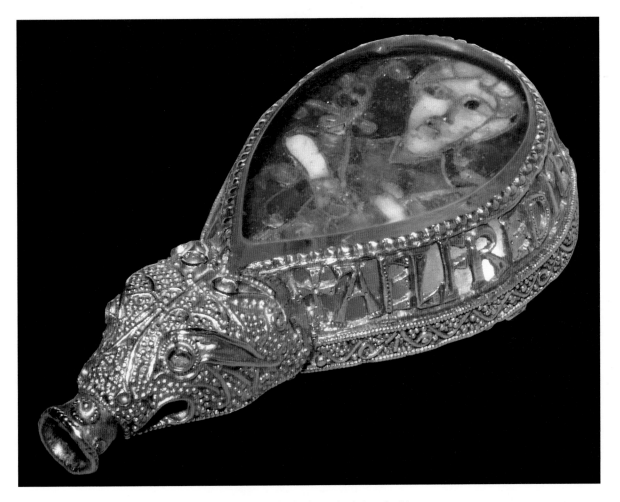

The Alfred Jewel which inspired the television episode The Wolvercote Tongue

under a piece of rock crystal enclosed in a gold frame. Around the edge was the inscription *Aelfred mec heht gewyrcan*, which translates as 'Alfred ordered me to be made'.

Very few of these costly give-aways have survived. In 1693, a well-preserved example was discovered in Somerset, four miles from Athelney where Alfred had founded a monastery. The artefact, known as the Alfred Jewel, is now a popular and priceless exhibit in the Ashmolean Museum's Dark Ages and early medieval collection.

Fronting on to Beaumont Street, and surmounted by a statue of Apollo, the Ashmolean is the oldest museum in Britain, pre-dating the British Museum by sixty years. As a policeman, Morse was amused to learn its history – it was founded not only on serious skulduggery and a highly suspicious death, but involved a notorious theft.

By right, the museum should be called the 'Tradescantian' in honour of John Tradescant and his son, also called John. Enthusiastic early seventeenth-century travellers, the pair built up a bizarre collection of curiosities known as 'Tradescant's Ark'. Originally displayed in Lambeth, where it was open to the public, the collection contained such oddities as Oliver Cromwell's death mask, Guy Fawkes' lantern and a piece of the stake at which the Oxford martyr Bishop Latimer was burned to death.

During the 1650s, father and son were befriended by Elias Ashmole, a former Brasenose College student, who persuaded John Tradescant senior to bequeath the entire collection to him, after John junior's death. Tradescant junior must have had second thoughts because when he died in 1662, his will stated the 'Ark' should pass first to his widowed mother and then to either Oxford or Cambridge University.

Ashmole's legal battle to enforce the deed of gift dragged on for ten years. To apply more pressure, he moved into the house next door to the obstinate Mrs Tradescant and attempted, verbally and physically, to harass her into submission. The courts finally backed his claim when it was discovered that Mrs Tradescant had been selling off the collection's choicest items to finance her lavish lifestyle. A few days later she was found drowned in her garden pond.

Oxford University was offered what remained of 'Tradescant's Ark' on condition it was displayed in a suitably impressive building. For much of the eighteenth century the collection languished in the first Ashmolean Museum in Broad Street where, in 1776, it attracted the attention of Jean-Paul Marat, a future leader of the French Revolution, and later the victim of a notorious murder. Marat helped himself to a gold chain and was eventually caught and sentenced to five years on a prison hulk.

In *The Wolvercote Tongue* – and later *The Jewel That Was Ours* – Dr Theodore Kemp was the Keeper of Anglo-Saxon and Medieval Antiquities at the Ashmolean. It was to Kemp that Laura Stratton, a tourist from California, had arranged to hand over the Wolvercote Jewel during her brief stay in Oxford. Within forty-eight hours both were dead and the Saxon artefact was missing. Mrs Stratton died of an apparent coronary in her hotel bedroom and the historian and lecturer at the hands of a murderer.

The Ashmolean Museum was founded on intrigue and sudden death which is equal to any Morse novel

A few yards south down St Aldate's is another historic building, which plays a significant part in both deaths.

Tea dances are still regularly held in the Assembly Room of Oxford Town Hall. During the Second World War, hundreds of GIs descended on the Friday night dances in their quest for 'local talent' and the promise of a brief carnal adventure in the University Parks. By coincidence, former American veterans Phil Aldrich, Eddie Stratton and Howard Brown – all tea-dance Lotharios – find themselves reunited for an Historic Cities of England tour. While being questioned over the death of his wife, Stratton confesses his part in a second reunion – with an Oxford woman he met and seduced after a 1944 town hall hop.

Although mentioned only briefly in *The Jewel That Was Ours*, the town hall would have played an important part in Morse's police career. Within the building is a court room used for magistrates' court hearings, Quarter Sessions and finally as a Crown Court until a new court complex was opened in 1985. As a senior officer, Morse would have attended the hearings to deliver his prosecution evidence.

Various forms of civic building can be traced to the town-hall site as far back as the thirteenth century. In 1229, Henry III sold the burgesses a house on the east side of St Aldate's on condition it be used as a court room. By 1550, the freehold of an adjoining house was acquired and converted into the lower Guildhall until, exactly 200 years later, both buildings were demolished and a new town hall erected.

As Victorian Oxford grew, so did the demands of its civic servants. By the summer of 1893, the old town hall had been demolished, leaving the fourteenth- and fifteenth-century crypt intact. The present town hall was officially opened ten months later by the Prince of Wales, later Edward VII. Originally used to house the city's central library, the southern corner of the surviving building now contains the Museum of Oxford which, in 1997, staged an Inspector Morse exhibition.

At Sunday school, Morse remembered asking his middle-aged and unimaginative teacher exactly where heaven was. It was a question his grammar school divinity teacher also failed to answer. 'If God created the Universe,' pestered the teenager, 'who in turn had created God?'

> Morse was a believer neither in the existence of God nor in the fixity of the Fates. About such things he never quite knew what he should think; and, like Hardy's, his philosophy of life amounted to little more than a heap of confused impressions, akin to those of a bewildered young boy at a conjuring show.

Oxford Town Hall dominates St Aldate's and is mentioned in The Jewel That Was Ours

Colin Dexter pulls off his own illusion in *Service of All the Dead* when he merges two city-centre churches to create the highly believable church of St Frideswide. The invention is even more credible because, as the patron saint of Oxford, St Frideswide is the one city church you would expect to find. Morse is on his way to the Ashmolean Museum when he alights from a bus in Cornmarket Street, outside the church of St Frideswide. From there, Morse would have been able to see the two churches his creator used as his models – St Michael-by-the-North-Gate on Cornmarket and St Mary Magdalen less than 200 yards further up on Magdalen Street.

Of the two churches, St Michael is the more historic. Its eleventh-century Saxon tower is the oldest surviving building in Oxford. St Mary Magdalen – known to Town and Gown alike as 'St Mary Mags' – occupies an island shared with the Martyrs' Memorial and is a mixture of medieval and Gothic-revival architecture.

'I don't like this kind of church,' Morse admits to his sergeant. He is talking of St Frideswide's, but his aversion to High Church trappings could well apply to St Mary Magdalen, where the congregation remains loyal to the memory of Charles I. Each year, on 30 January, it celebrates the Feast of King Charles the Martyr.

It was while Morse was on an eight-week secondment to west Africa in the autumn of 1976 that the St Frideswide's churchwarden Harry Josephs was murdered. Three weeks later, the Reverend Lionel

St Mary Magdalen – one of the two churches Colin Dexter combines to create St Frideswide in Service of All the Dead

Lawson fell to his death from the church's tower. In *Service of All the Dead*, six months later, during an 'empty two-week furlough', Morse drags Lewis from an Oxford United football match to help with unofficial investigation.

The pair ascend St Frideswide's tower – Lewis climbing, Morse crawling – to discover the body of a third victim. A few days later, the pair descend into the crypt to find the church's fourth victim, this time a young schoolboy. After chasing and cornering the murderer at the top of the same tower, Morse is saved from almost certain death by his sergeant.

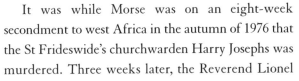

St Michael's eleventh-century Saxon tower is the oldest surviving building in Oxford.

Following in the footsteps first of Colin Dexter on one of his research expeditions around the city, and then of two of his suspects, will lead us not surprisingly to even more churches. Dexter likes churches. You never know, he candidly admits, what you will find there.

Six days after her husband was found murdered in annexe 3 of Oxford's Haworth Hotel, Margaret Bowman parks her car in St Giles' and sets off down Magdalen Street. At the corner of Cornmarket and Queen Streets she tries the door of Carfax Tower. Shut. There was always the spire of St Mary the Virgin.

> A few minutes later she was standing in Radcliffe Square; and as she looked up
> at the north side of St Mary's Church, a strange and fatal fascination seemed to
> grip her soul.

A few flights of wide wooden steps lead up to the main landing. A notice on a locked door to the left advises visitors that this was the Old Library – the very first one belonging to the University – where the few books amassed by the earliest scholars were so precious that they were chained to the walls. The stairs – iron now, and no longer enclosed for the next two flights – lead up and over the roof of the Lady Chapel, and she feels a sense of exhilaration in the cold air as she climbs higher still to the Bell Tower.

> For several seconds as she emerged at the top of the tower, Margaret was
> conscious of a terrifying giddiness as her eyes glimpsed, just below her feet, the
> black iron ring that circled the golden-painted Roman numerals of the great
> clock adorning the north wall of the church. But the panic was gone, and she
> looked out across at the Radcliffe Camera; and then to the left of Camera at the
> colleges along Broad Street; then the buildings of Balliol where Cranmer had
> redeemed his soul amid the burning brushwood; then she could see the leafless
> trees along St Giles'...

Imminent death is nothing new to the tower of the university church of St Mary the Virgin. On the Feast of St Scholastica in 1355, the bell of St Mary's was rung by the students – the townsmen used the bells of Carfax Tower – as a call to arms after a brawl in the Swindlestock Tavern in St Aldate's escalated into a full-scale battle. The site of the Swindlestock Tavern, which closed in 1709, is marked by an inscription on the Abbey National Bank.

Long before the construction of the Old Schools or the Sheldonian Theatre or the Bodleian, St Mary's was considered the administrative and educational heart of Oxford University. Its 188ft tower, which Margaret Bowman climbed with purpose, dates from the late thirteenth century. Inside, theological dogma and intolerance add historic spice to the otherwise dull architecture.

In 1553, with the Roman Catholic Queen Mary on the throne, the Protestant bishops Thomas Cranmer (Archbishop of Canterbury), Hugh Latimer (Bishop of Worcester) and Nicholas Ridley (Bishop of London), all Cambridge men, were brought for trial to the more conservative Oxford. By 1556, Latimer and Ridley had both died at the stake. Cranmer was granted time to recant his support of the Protestant Reformation and signed several new statements. Queen Mary was not satisfied and ordered Cranmer to confess his errors publicly in St Mary's. His refusal sealed his fate. While the archbishop languished in jail, workmen set about cutting back and turning one of the church pillars into a 'court dock'. It was from this stunted pillar, which can still be seen opposite the pulpit on the north side of the nave, that Cranmer faced his final trial.

In 1833, St Mary the Virgin was once again the seat of controversy when John Keble delivered a sermon calling for the foundation of the Anglo-Catholic Oxford Movement. His plea found both religious and ridiculous support.

John Henry Newman, the vicar of St Mary's, was increasingly attacked for his pro-Catholic views. Some colleges even changed the times of compulsory chapel services to keep students from hearing Newman's reactionary sermons. Those students seduced by his arguments dressed ascetically, fasted on water and toast and smoked only Spanish 'Catholic' cigars. Newman eventually resigned and became a Catholic Cardinal. Oxford remained the seat of High Church Anglo-Catholicism.

The Martyrs' Memorial – at the head of St Giles' and outside Balliol College – is rarely mentioned, but remains a passing feature in nearly all of Colin Dexter's stories. Built on the site of the Robin Hood Inn and carved by Henry Weekes, the monument has three statues – Cranmer facing north and holding a Bible dated May 1541, the year the Bible was freely circulated by royal authority; Ridley facing east; and Latimer facing west with his arms crossed and head bowed. On the wall of Balliol college is an inscription to the martyrs and opposite the plaque, in the centre of Broad Street, is an iron cross marking the spot where the executions took place.

Morse walked or drove past the monument most days. In *The Jewel That Was Ours*, the American tourists staying at The Randolph Hotel overlook the memorial. Howard Brown excuses himself from a city tour, which starts at the monument, to visit the far more interesting Didcot Railway Museum, a decision that Morse would quite probably have agreed with.

There was another absentee suspect. Questioned by Morse over Laura Stratton's death, John Ashenden finally admits disappearing to visit Holywell Cemetery, north east of the city centre. Leaving The Randolph, the tour guide...

... crossed over by the Martyrs' Memorial into Broad Street. The sun no longer slanted across the pale-yellow stone, the early evening was becoming much cooler, and he was wearing a lightweight raincoat. He strode fairly quickly past the front of Balliol, the great gates of Trinity, Blackwell's Book Shop... Even more briskly now, Ashenden walked past the King's Arms, the Holywell Music Room, the back of New College – until he came to Longwall Street. Here he turned left; and after two hundred yards or so went through the wooden gate that led to Holywell Cemetery.

It was here, in the nearby St Cross Church, Holywell, that the church interior scenes for the television adaptation of *Service of All the Dead* were shot.

The cemetery where Ashenden searched out the grave of an old friend has artistic connections of its own. Here, as Colin Dexter lists in *The Jewel That Was Ours*, are the gravestones of Kenneth Grahame, the author of *Wind in the Willows*; Sir John Stainer, the composer; and the critic, Ken Tynan.

Morse's own re-acquaintance with dead bodies invariably meant – at least, in the first ten novels – a reunion with Max de Bryn, the hump-backed police surgeon. In *The Jewel That Was Ours*, the Chief Inspector is called to the banks of the River Cherwell to be greeted by

Max's thespian turn of phrase. "'The dead man lay there, Morse,' said Max pointing to the water at the head of the weir, "'something pale and long and white', as the young lady said.'"

The corpse, as Morse knew only too well, was that of Dr Theodore Kemp, the ostentatious and lascivious

left: Holywell Cemetery which provides an alibi for John Ashenden in The Jewel That Was Ours

right: Rarely mentioned in the novels, the Martyrs' Memorial provides an historic backdrop for most of the television episodes

over: The Rainbow Bridge spans the River Cherwell in University Parks

MAGDALEN STREET

Ashmolean curator. Parson's Pleasure was a fittingly named place for such a philanderer to end his days.

Approached through the University Parks, Parson's Pleasure is a secluded stretch of the River Cherwell where, tradition has it, individuals and groups of men are allowed to swim naked without fear of social or legal persecution.

This famous and infamous bathing place is to be found at a point where the Cherwell adapts itself into a pleasingly circumscribed swimming area at a bend of the river, with a terrace of unsophisticated, though adequate, cubicles enabling would-be bathers to shed their clothing and to don, or not to don, their swimming costumes there. Green-painted, corrugated-iron fencing surrounds Parson's Pleasure, with the access gate fairly jealously guarded during the summer months, and firmly locked after the waters are deemed too cold even for the doughtiest of its homoerotic habitues.

The custom was, apparently, so well founded that even straitlaced Victorian women accepted the need to disembark from their punts and walk around the rear of the pool to avoid the sight of naked sunbathers. A second, ladies-only spa, called 'Dame's Delight' was opened in 1934 but was forced to close in 1970 because of flood damage.

The University Parks has its own twilight history – 'the setting for countless copulations since Royalist artillery was quartered on its acres during the Civil War'. Three centuries later, during the Second World War, countless American soldiers and airmen attempted to coax their British girlfriends towards the Parks and the tree-screened privacy of Parson's Pleasure in the hope of consummating international relations. As a GI awaiting his D-Day posting, Howard Brown took his lover Betty Fowler there and, reunited forty-seven years later, admits to Morse to returning to the same spot for a 'quiet little kiss and cuddle'.

In his book *Oxford and Cambridge*, comparing the two, J.J. Smithfield-Waterstone claims: 'Cambridge has espoused the river, has opened its arms to the river, has built some of its finest houses alongside the river. Oxford has turned its back on the river, for only at some points downstream from Folly Bridge does the Isis glitter so gloriously as does the Cam.'

The real difference, as Colin Dexter points out in *The Daughters of Cain*, is that the Thames – and its tributary the Cherwell – have been viewed by the residents of Oxford more as recreation than real estate:

> The two rivers, the Thames (or Isis) and the Cherwell, making their confluence just to the south of the city centre, have long provided enjoyable amenities for Oxford folk, both Town and Gown: punting, rowing, sculling, canoeing, and pleasure-boating. For the less athletic, and for the more arthritic, the river cruise down from Folly Bridge via the Iffley and Sandford locks to Abingdon, has always been a favourite.

It is from the upper deck of a pleasure boat, the *Iffley Princess*, that a young passenger spots the body of Edward Brooks floating in the Thames just below the concrete arch of Donnington Bridge.

To Oxford residents and pedantics such as Morse, the city's largest river would always be the Isis, a Latinate name first used in 1535 by John Leland who, for some unrecorded reason, was unhappy with the pre-Roman Celtic name – *tam* from 'broad' and *wys* meaning water. To the rest of the world, it remains the River Thames.

Literary Mysteries

Oxford Gazette: The first real newspaper, other than a newsletter, to be published in England. It appeared in November 1665, the court being then at Oxford owing to the great plague, and was started by H. Muddiman under the direction of his patron Sir Joseph Williamson. It became the London Gazette in 1666.

THE OXFORD COMPANION TO ENGLISH LITERATURE

IMAGINE A PSYCHOLOGIST conducting a word-association test. It is sometime in the early 1970s and his next word is 'Oxford'. The most common response is 'University'. From then on, answers vary with social class and educational background. Graduates, Oxford or otherwise, might well be expected to answer 'blue' or 'movement'. Avid readers or crossword fanatics will almost certainly respond with 'dictionary', while the majority of manual and factory workers dig no deeper than the Oxford and Cambridge boat race.

Fast forward twenty years to the mid-1990s. This time there is a quite different response. For the majority of people, 'Oxford' has come to mean just one thing – Chief Inspector Morse.

This is not just a British phenomenon. An Australian psychology journal claimed the 'impregnation of Inspector Morse on the public psyche' is the 'most important and far-reaching influence ever exerted by a fictional character' in literary history. In fact, Morse's association with Oxford has become so challenging that one year the city's Playhouse Theatre went as far as hiring billboards to announce: 'Inspector Morse is no longer Oxford's only decent drama.'

There is no doubt Morse would have been successful wherever Colin Dexter chose to employ his talents, but surely there is more to it than that? Morse, after all, is an Oxford animal. 'Once you're taken to the University's bosom,' he warned Sergeant Lewis in *The Last Enemy*, 'you're preserved like Sleeping Beauty in a rarefied atmosphere of hot air and alcohol. Ageing is unknown.'

Oxford, as Colin Dexter freely admits, has such a physical presence in the books and television films that it has assumed the role of an extra 'character'. A Morse story is moulded by the buildings and the weather as well as by the actions of its characters. In fact, the people sometimes appear to be props in the setting rather than characters in the plot. Its stunning architecture, tight streets and historic buildings give Oxford a unique old English ambience; a city it may be, but it feels more like a village community.

Psychologists might well pounce on another sub-conscious link. Why should Oxford, a city founded on academic books, earn so much of its reputation from popular crime novels?

'The detective novel,' claims the essayist George Grella, 'is for ever popular because it provides the reader with a means of escape from the harsh realities of everyday life. Mystery fiction is a literary release valve for millions of people who are perfectly willing to suspend their disbelief and become a part of an intricate tale of murder.'

Armchair detectives fall into two distinct camps. There are those who consider themselves intellectually inferior to the investigator – not difficult with a Morse novel – and admit their biggest pleasure comes from observing the detective at work; and those who love mysteries, not because of the puzzle, but because it gives them a page-by-page chance to out-think the detective.

Morse was not the first detective to solve the murders of Oxford, nor Colin Dexter the first crime writer to live and be inspired by the city's malevolent beauty.

A year or two before his 1978 death, the crime writer Edmund Crispin read *Last Bus to Woodstock*. The next day he wrote to the book's publisher complaining that in the novel Sergeant Lewis had acted with 'commendable promptitude' when he could quite easily have acted 'quickly'. Colin Dexter considered a correction for a future edition, but rejected a change because he 'didn't think that would be right'.

The pedantic Crispin – real name Robert Bruce Montgomery – had another reason for reading Dexter's first novel with over-zealous care. A quarter of a century earlier, Crispin was one of Britain's best-read crime writers, with a hero who walked the same streets and drank in the same pubs as Chief Inspector Morse.

Montgomery was born at Chesham Bois, Buckinghamshire in 1921, the son of Scots–Irish parents, and inherited his ancestors' roving spirit. After leaving the Merchant Taylor's School in London he announced, much to his parents' disapproval, that he intended touring Europe before attending university. Four years later he received his BA in modern languages from St John's College – where Morse studied seven years later – before working as a schoolmaster at Shrewsbury School. His friend, the poet and novelist and fellow St John's graduate Philip Larkin, worked nearby and the pair read each other's manuscripts.

As an undergraduate, Montgomery had read John Dickson Carr's novel *The Crooked Hinge*. It drastically altered his view of crime stories and inspired him to create his own

detective hero. The following year, 1944, 'Edmund Crispin' published his first novel – *The Case of the Gilded Fly: Obsequies at Oxford* – and introduced the world to Gervase Fen, a cynical university professor partly based on the Oxford don W.E. Moore.

Fen is Oxford's only other detective hero and he features in a series of nine fast-paced, tongue-in-cheek crime mysteries. 'The Gervase Fen novels are a blend of John Dickson Carr, Michael Innes, M.R. James and the Marx Brothers,' claimed the critic Anthony Boucher.

For a more philosophical comment, we need to read Julian Symons in *Bloody Murder*: 'Crispin's work is marked by a highly individual sense of light comedy, and by a great flair for verbal deception rather in the Christie manner... At his weakest he is flippant, at his best he is witty, but all his work shows a high-spiritedness rare and welcome in the crime story.'

Morse's only Oxford rival is Edmund Crispin's cynical professor-detective Gervase Fen

Physically and mentally, Fen and Morse are beyond comparison. They do share a love of poetry and literature, but Morse is closer to Inspector Humbley, a policeman who invariably cooperates with the sleuthing don. He wants to discuss literature constantly and is disgusted by the continual criminal interruptions.

One can only imagine what Morse would have made of Fen's flamboyant dress and childlike enthusiasm. A professor of English language and literature, Fen is tall, about forty, with a cheerful, clean-shaven face and dark hair plastered down with water. Usually he wears an enormous raincoat with extraordinary hats. Fen is happily married and drives a red roadster. His favourite expostulations – 'Oh, my paws!' and 'Oh, my furs and whiskers!' – come from Lewis Carroll.

The plot of Crispin's most famous 'rococo' mystery, *The Moving Toyshop* – voted by H.R.F. Keating as among the best one hundred crime stories ever written – would have intrigued Colin Dexter's detective. The poet Richard Cadogan arrives in Oxford for a holiday and finds a dead woman in a room above a toyshop. He is knocked unconscious and when he comes round the woman's body has disappeared and the toyshop has turned into a grocery store. The police do not believe Cadogan's story and the poet contacts Gervase Fen, who immediately finds a clue – a telephone number scribbled on a piece of paper.

The last Gervase Fen mystery, *Fen Country*, was published in 1979, a year after the author's death. By then, Bruce Montgomery had earned himself another niche in popular culture. After learning to play the piano as a teenager, Montgomery went on to compose several orchestral and choral works. In the late 1950s, he expanded his output to include songs and film scores – including several for the 'Carry On' series.

Nigel Strangeways, another Oxford-educated sleuth, created by Wadham College graduate and future Poet Laureate Cecil Day Lewis, is a detective after Morse's heart. With pale-blue eyes and a sardonic turn of humour, he frequently quotes from Blake and Keats, and Morse's particular favourite, A.E. Housman.

As a postgraduate, Day Lewis worked as a schoolmaster. In 1935, he decided to supplement his income from poetry by writing a crime novel; he needed the money to repair the roof of a cottage he was living in. His literary agent offered him one piece of advice and that was to keep his roles as poet and detective novelist quite separate. So Cecil Day Lewis became Nicholas Blake. His first book, *A Question of Proof*, was followed by nineteen more crime novels, at least three-quarters of which feature the enigmatic Nigel Strangeways.

Of fictional characters, Morse has only one hero and cites Sherlock Holmes on several occasions:

Sherlock Holmes:
Morse's fictional detective hero

> 'You remember your Sherlock Holmes, Lewis? – "Is there any point to which
>   you would wish to draw my attention?"
> "To the curious incident of the dog in the night-time."
> "The dog did nothing in the night-time."
> "That was the curious incident."'

But more often than not Lewis, whose teenage reading did not include *A Study in Scarlet* or *The Valley of Fear*, did not remember.

In his excellent book *The World of Inspector Morse*, Christopher Bird explains how Conan Doyle's character and Morse differ in their deductive approach:

> Both men insist on cerebration as a means of solving crimes, both resort to
> psychoactive substances (though Morse takes not a 7 per cent solution of cocaine
> but a pint or three of cask-conditioned beer) and both are bachelors – though in
> Morse's case not without occasional regrets. However, the big difference between
> Morse and Holmes is in 'method'. Holmes is big on deduction, backed up by keen
> observation, research and record keeping. Morse has the police computer
> whenever he wants it, but his method of making random connections to see where
> they lead – 'blundering about' he calls it – would be anathema to Holmes.

By some puzzle of fate, Oxford has produced three of the best – and best-selling – crime writers of the twentieth century. Two were born in the city; the third has made it his adopted home.

On the wall of No. 1 Brewer Street, off St Aldate's and south of Pembroke College, is a plaque marking the birthplace of Dorothy L. Sayers, the doyenne of inter-war crime writers. At the time of his only daughter's birth on 13 June 1893, the Reverend Henry Sayers was head-master of Christ Church Cathedral School. The family soon departed and it was not until 1912 that Dorothy Sayers returned to Oxford with a scholarship to study at Somerville College.

She obtained a first in modern languages but had to wait another five years to graduate while the University debated whether women should be allowed to receive degrees. Dismayed at the delay and at the prospect of academic life, Dorothy joined the publishing staff of Blackwell's bookshop. In 1922, she left Oxford once more, this time for a job with Bensons, the London advertising agency.

During the day, Sayers wrote advertisement and poster copy for some of the best-selling products of the post-war years. At night, she was writing her first crime novel, *Whose Body*, in which she introduced her aristocratic hero Lord Peter Wimsey. Fourteen more Wimsey

No 1 Brewer Street: birthplace of crime writer Dorothy L. Sayers

novels and a clutch of short stories followed, ultimately earning Sayers the presidency of the Detection Club. Her final Wimsey mystery, *Gaudy Night*, was published in 1935 after which she concentrated on writing stage and radio dramas.

When P.D. James first thought of writing a crime novel it was more through financial need than a desire to make her hero different from the classic 'gentlemanly amateur' detective. She created Chief Inspector (later Commander) Adam Dalgliesh, a dedicated and efficient policeman and respected poet.

Phyllis Dorothy James was born in Oxford in 1920, the eldest of three children and the daughter of an inland-revenue officer. Her education ended when she was sixteen. At the conclusion of the Second World War she was married with two daughters of her own and forced to care for her battle-scarred and schizophrenic doctor husband who spent the next nineteen years in various mental institutions.

Money was extremely tight and James not only managed to qualify from evening classes, but worked her way up through the Civil Service. In 1968, and already a published author, she became a Principal in the Home Office criminal policy unit – fertile pickings for her crime thrillers.

Made a life peer in 1991 and an honorary fellow of St Hilda's College, Oxford, five years later, James is now one of Britain's most prolific crime writers. She is also adept at weaving a cross-thread of characters from book to book. Adam Dalgliesh appears in twelve books, so far. Two more books feature Cordelia Gray whose mentor and one-time boss, Bernie, once worked with Dalgliesh in the CID. In later stories, it is two of the senior detective's sergeants, Piers Tarrant and Kate Miskin, who become embroiled in still more mysteries.

Surprisingly, Oxford's most famous living author claims he has never been a full-time crime writer – 'If you only write a page a day that's 365 pages a year or one-and-a-half books.' Ever modest, Colin Dexter attributes the creation and initial success of his Inspector Morse novels to lousy weather and a bout of flu.

After graduating from Cambridge in 1953, Dexter became a teacher. His classroom career ended in 1966 when his progressive deafness forced his retirement from teaching, and he moved to Oxford where he joined the staff of the University Examination Board.

'In 1972 I was on holiday in North Wales and it was raining,' explains Dexter, 'and when the children had finished complaining I hadn't much to do. I had a tedious day ahead. I'd read all the books that were there and thought I might be able to write a crime novel as good as the lousy one I'd just finished, so I sat down and wrote the first chapter of *Last Bus to Woodstock*. It wasn't more than four or five pages, the holiday finished and I forgot all about it.'

He did not reread his first-chapter draft for another six months, and then he carried on with the story each evening after work between listening to 'The Archers' and his nightly visit to a local pub.

The first publishing house to read the manuscript returned it with a six-page letter of suggested improvements. Dexter posted it, without making any changes, to a second publisher. George Hardinge – Lord Hardinge of Penshurst – was in charge of Macmillan's crime catalogue and took *Last Bus to Woodstock* home to read while recovering from influenza. Macmillan has remained Dexter's publisher ever since and the author has repaid Hardinge's faith by using his name for at least four separate characters in his books.

There are many similarities between Morse and his creator. Both are Latin and Greek classicists. 'He was rather like Athena,' admits Dexter, 'who sprang fully grown and fully blown from the head of Zeus.'

The inspiration for his name came from Sir Jeremy Morse, the early 1970s chairman

of Lloyds Bank. Morse is an old Oxfordshire name and Sir Jeremy was a compulsive crossword solver and clue writer. 'I have always enjoyed people with a cerebral quickness,' says Dexter.

Morse, like his creator, uses his daily crossword – sometimes three or four a day – as a form of mental keep fit. Each morning he buys a copy of *The Times* and, leaving the news and features pages unread, turns immediately to the crossword:

> 1 Across: Code name for a walrus (5). Ha! The clue was like a megaphone
> shouting the answer at him. It was going to be his day!

It was not unusual for Lewis to find his superior irate and scratchy after completing all but one of *The Times* clues in little more than six minutes. 'Seldom was it that he failed to finish things off, and that within a pretty smartish time, too. All he needed was a large scotch…and the answer (he knew) would hit him straight between the eyes.'

Throughout the 1970s and '80s, Morse bought a copy of the now defunct *Listener* magazine. Only the penultimate page and its convoluted crossword held Morse's attention – and then only for a few minutes.

While Morse may have disparaged his sergeant's devotion to the *Sunday* and *Daily Mirror*, his own Sunday newspaper order always included a copy of the *News of the World*. Its sexual revelations provided a lightweight interlude to the crossword set by Azed, for Morse the 'Kasparov of cruciverbalists' and the natural successor to the eminent Ximenes in the *Observer*.

Apart from the first experimental pages of *Last Bus to Woodstock*, the process of producing a Morse novel has never changed. Colin Dexter works at a desk in the first-floor study of his North Oxford house – just yards from where Morse sits at his own desk.

'I write in longhand, in biro,' explains Dexter. 'The first draft is very rough. I just go through the story from A to B. That's the hard work. Then I write it all out again in a more orderly and ordered form. Finally, I go through it once more, give it a bit of tarting up, then send it off to be typed by someone else.'

To Dexter, a story – any story – needs a sense of place. 'I never do anything without an enormous amount of topographical research in Oxford,' he says. But there is more to it than simple legwork. Dexter uses his city perambulations equally as inspiration and investigation. 'The Romans had a motto, *solvitur ambulando*,' he explains, 'which roughly translates to "walk about to work it out". If you sit passively and just wait for something to happen, you're unlikely to write very much.'

It was on one of these walks that Dexter discovered the war memorial in Bonn Square in the heart of Oxford, just yards from the city's Westgate Shopping Centre. Reading the list of casualties, he found that one young soldier, killed by Ugandan mutineers in 1897, had the unusual surname of Death. The experience was not wasted. In *Service of All the Dead*, a group of alcoholic tramps make the same odd find.

Occasionally, Morse and Lewis make their own historical discoveries. In *Death is Now My Neighbour*, the pair drive over to North Oxford to question Julian Storrs, the flashy anthropologist and Master of Lonsdale contender, in his own home. Lewis had backed into the first available space in Polstead Road, the tree-lined thoroughfare that leads westward from Woodstock Road into Jericho:

> The houses here were of a pattern: gabled, red-bricked, three-storeyed
>   properties, with ashlared, mullioned windows, the frames universally
>   painted white; interesting and amply proportioned houses built towards the
>   end of the nineteenth century.
> 'Seen that before, Sir?' Lewis pointed to the circular blue plaque on the wall
>   opposite: This house was the home of T.E. Lawrence (Lawrence of Arabia)
>   from 1896–1921.
> Morse grunted as he straightened up his aching back, mumbling of lumbago.

The Polstead Road former home of T. E. Lawrence is
mentioned in Death is Now My Neighbour

An archaeological scholar, adventurer, military strategist, writer and, in turn, an army officer and a lowly airman in the Royal Air Force, T.E. Lawrence has more than anything survived as one of the legendary heroes of the First World War. His dashing attempts to help the Arabs against the Turks – portrayed in the 1962 film – made him famous in his lifetime as Lawrence of Arabia.

At grammar school, Morse had read Lawrence's *Seven Pillars of Wisdom*, but books, at least until his tenth birthday, were kept strictly to the practical and minimum. The single short bookshelf on which the family library stood supported just four works: *The Life of Captain Cook* (his father's); a 1910 edition of *The Family Doctor* (his mother's); *A Pictorial History of the Great War* (of which his father never spoke), and *Chamber's Dictionary*. The latter was exclusively young Morse's. Reading late into the night, he would tiptoe through the sleeping house to look up a new or unfamiliar word.

Each week a copy of the *Dandy* comic would be delivered with his father's morning paper and each month a *Meccano Magazine*. It left him with several childhood and childish fascinations: model train sets; railway engines and steam trains; and the engineering achievements of Isambard Kingdom Brunel.

There were other magazines – and the beginnings of guilt. While he was in Lower IVA, an increasingly smudged and grubby copy of *Naturist Journal* had done the rounds. When it was his turn, he locked and bolted every door in the house, even though he knew his parents were out and not expected home for some time.

Years later, in *The Wench is Dead*, Morse was hospitalised with a perforated ulcer and attempted to occupy his time and his mind with the mildly pornographic novel, *The Blue Ticket*. It was not enough. Ever hungry for a mystery to solve, Morse enlisted the daughter of a fellow patient to help discover the truth about a nineteenth-century murder, detailed in another book he was given, *Murder on the Oxford Canal*. Perhaps the clues he sought were buried somewhere in Oxford's Bodleian Library.

The Bodleian is the largest academic library in the world and contains six million books and one million maps. As one of the country's three copyright libraries – the others are the British Library in London and Cambridge University Library – the Bodleian is entitled to receive a copy of every book published in the United Kingdom. It also archives thousands of documents and manuscripts, most of which are stored underground in eighty miles of tunnels and in the much larger New Bodleian.

The Old Schools Quadrangle and home of the original Bodleian Library

Built in 1939 on the corner of Broad Street and Parks Road, the New Bodleian's fortress-like frontage provides the entrance to three floors of underground storage beneath the adjoining Blackwell's bookshop. A tunnel with a conveyor belt beneath Broad Street links the new site with the original Bodleian in the Old Schools Quadrangle.

It was among this labyrinth of documents that Christine Greenaway attempted to answer Morse's obscure and apparently senseless queries. The senior Bodleian librarian makes her way to work, her thoughts disturbed by the hospital patient she had met the previous evening:

> Such self-admonition prevailed as she walked that morning down the Broad, past Balliol and Trinity on her left, before crossing over the road, just before Blackwell's, and proceeding, *sub imperatoibus*, up the semi-circular steps into the gravelled courtyard of the Sheldonian. Thence, keeping to her right, she walked past the SILENCE PLEASE notice under the archway, and came out at last into her real home territory – the Quadrangle of the Schools... Over the months and years, though, she had gradually grown over-familiar with what the postcards on sale in the Proscholium still called 'The Golden Heart of Oxford'; grown familiar, as she regularly trod the gravelled quad, with the Tower of the Five Orders to her left, made her way past the bronze statue of the third Earl of Pembroke, and entered the Bodleian Library through the great single doorway in the West side, beneath the four tiers of blind arches in their gloriously mellowed stone.

In the final quarter of the fifteenth century, Duke Humphrey of Gloucester, brother of Henry V, donated a collection of books to the city of Oxford. The books were housed in rooms over the Divinity School until several of the most important volumes were 'borrowed' by Edward VI. It was a lesson that future custodians would not forget. In 1602 Thomas Bodley, the Ambassador to the Netherlands, formed a new library and insisted that no book may be taken away – no matter what the status of the lender.

During the Civil War, Charles I retreated from the battle of Naseby and sought refuge in Oxford. Seeking guidance on his situation, the king sent a note to the keepers of the Bodleian Library, informing them he wanted to study a book on other civil wars. His request was denied. The Bodleian, King Charles was politely informed, never lends books – not even to royalty. When the doomed king fled the city, the library demonstrated its equanimity by refusing a similar request from Oliver Cromwell.

The Bodleian Library: Kenneth Graham bequeathed the copyright and royalties of The Wind in the Willows *to the library*

Daniel Defoe continues the story of the library's expansion in his 1720s *A Tour Through the Whole of Great Britain*:

> In this state of things, one Sir Thomas Bodley, a wealthy and learned knight, zealous for the encouragment both of learning and religion, resolv'd to apply both his time, and estate, to erecting and furnishing a new library for the publick use of the University.
>
> In this good and charitable undertaking, he went on so successfully, for so many years, and with such a profusion of expence, and obtain'd such assistances from all the encouragers of learning in his time, that having collected books and manuscripts from all parts of the learned world; he got leave of the University, (and well they might grant it) to place them in the old library room, built as is said, by the good Duke Humphry.
>
> To this great work, great additions have been since made in books, as well as contributions in money, and more are added every day; and thus the work was brought to a head, the 8th of Nov. 1602, and has continued encreasing by the benefactions of great and learned men to this day: to remove the books once more and place them in beauty and splendor suitable to so glorious a collection, the late Dr Radcliff has left a legacy of £40,000 say some, others say not quite so much, to the building a new repository or library for the use of the University: this work is yet built, but I am told 'tis likely to be such a building as will be a greater ornament to the place than any yet standing in it.

The Bodleian also features in a Morse television episode – *Twilight of the Gods* – when an assassin uses one of the library's windows to fire into an honorary degree procession. Morse's favourite diva, Gwaldys Probert, is fatally wounded.

It has been claimed that Oxford's reputation is built on books, and one cornerstone of that status is Blackwell's bookshop. Morse was certainly a regular visitor. As a student he bought most of his textbooks there and as a policeman his wallet contained a Blackwell's discount card.

Blackwell's is such an important Oxford institution it is difficult to believe that it did not open its doors until 1879.

Justly proud of its title as Europe's biggest bookshop and its Guinness Book of Records entry for the world's largest display of books for sale in a single room – on more than three miles of shelving – Blackwell's beginnings were a little more modest.

Despite its august Broad Street neighbours – Trinity, Balliol, Exeter, Hertford and Wadham Colleges and Christopher Wren's Sheldonian Theatre – Benjamin Henry Blackwell's first shop was just 12ft square. It was situated opposite two well-established

*A mid-nineteenth century print of the Bodleian which
still enforces a rule that no books may leave the building*

competitors, which prompted Frederick Macmillan, the founder of the Macmillan publishing house, to remark: 'Well, Mr Blackwell, we shall be pleased to open an account with you but I fear you have chosen the wrong side of the street to be successful.'

The shop quickly expanded, partly because of its founder's dedication to books and his philosophy that selling them should be governed by an 'infinite capacity for taking pains'. He also established another Blackwell's tradition, still upheld today, that customers should be allowed to browse, unhurried and undisturbed by staff.

Blackwell's claims that every single student to have attended Oxford University during the twentieth century is more than likely to have purchased a book there. John Betjeman recorded his visit in 'Summoned by Bells':

> *I wandered into Blackwell's, where my bill*
> *Was so enormous that it wasn't paid*
> *Til ten years later, from the small estate*
> *My father left.*

In 1924, Benjamin Blackwell died and his position as company chairman was inherited by his son Basil, known affectionately, despite his subsequent

Blackwell's Bookshop where scenes in Who Killed Harry Field? *and* The Dead of Jericho *were filmed*

knighthood, as 'the Gaffer'. Under Sir Basil's guidance, Blackwell's continued its expansion, first into publishing and then opening more shops around the city. Today, Blackwell's has nine shops in Oxford. Its most impressive enlargement came in 1966 with the opening of the Norrington Room, a vast underground department constructed under the south-east corner of Trinity College.

Morse would pick up and read a book – sometimes a few pages, sometimes a complete chapter – according to his mood. He was, explains his creator, 'not a systematic reader, but a dipper-in'.

In *Last Seen Wearing*, we are informed that his bedside cabinet supported *The Selected Prose* of A.E. Housman, Ernest Newman's biography of Wagner, *Selected Stories* by Rudyard Kipling and John Livingstone Lowe's biography of the Romantic poet Coleridge, *The Road to Xanadu*. Which book he read, and for how long, depended on how busy his mind was.

Morse's literary hero A. E. Housman – like the detective, Housman studied at St John's and failed his finals

Literature – and books in general – are as much a part of Morse's life as the music that drifts through his flat. Whether at his home or visiting a friend or at the scene of a crime, scattered extracts from books prove tantalisingly distracting – 'He was reminded of a passage which had once been part of his mental baggage, the words of which now slowly returned to him.'

As a melancholy and sometimes suicidal teenager, Morse frequently sought refuge in his books, almost as if they were photographs in a treasured family album. For comfort he reread chapters from his favourite works: *Tess of the d'Urbervilles* or something from Dickens. Morse was convinced that *Bleak House* remained the greatest book ever written. For reassurance, and deliberately to annoy his stepmother, he turned to poetry: 'The Odyssey', Andrew Marvell or Housman. Poetry would always remain Morse's greatest passion. He was a committed – although not always active – member of the Oxford Book Association. In the early pages of *The Dead of Jericho*, he attends a meeting at the Clarendon Press Institute to hear the association's former Merton Professor of English Literature, Dame Helen Gardner, only because she is discussing her *New Oxford Book of Verse*.

As a student, Morse had once retraced a favourite river-path walk of Gerard Manley Hopkins. The poet had recorded his walk from Osney Bridge, where the Botley Road

---

Morse and Lewis spent an evening pondering the complexities of
The Secret of Annexe 3 *at the Eagle and Child*

crosses the Isis, up as far as Binsey – 'the wind-wandering, weed-winding bank' – and lamented the felling of aspens along the river bank in his 1879 poem 'Binsey Poplars'.

The same distance beyond Binsey brings you to the ruins of Godstow Nunnery and eventually to the Trout Inn at Wolvercote. In his more fanciful moments, Morse would sit on the Trout Inn verandah – 'drinking and thinking, thinking and drinking' – and imagine how much the literary world owed to this small triangle of Oxfordshire river bank.

It was here, seated beneath a hay rick, that, in order to pacify and amuse three excited sisters, a young Oxford deacon called Charles Dodgson created one of the greatest of all children's books, *Alice in Wonderland*. Was it the same grass Matthew Arnold's 'Scholar Gipsy' had helped harvest?

And, above Godstow Bridge, when hay-time's here
In June, and many a scythe in sunshine flames,
Men who through those wide fields of breezy grass
Where black-wing'd swallows haunt the glittering Thames,
To bathe in the abandon'd lasher pass,
Have often pass'd thee near
Sitting upon the river bank o'ergrown;
Mark'd thine outlandish garb, thy figure spare,
Thy dark vague eyes, and soft abstracted air—
But, when they came from bathing, thos wast gone!

In another pub, this time in the centre of Oxford, it was Lewis who imagined a more modest fantasy. The conversation had started with murder and somehow drifted into literature. Sitting in a snug at the Eagle and Child, Lewis sipped his orange juice and attempted to take in his boss's latest lesson.

Known fondly as the 'Bird and Babe', the public house in which they now sat had occupied the same St Giles' site since 1650; that much Lewis knew. Comforted by its homely fireside surroundings it was here, Morse continued, that the informal literary group known as the Inklings met for almost four decades until the 1960s. Its leader was C.S. Lewis – described by his pupil John Betjeman as 'breezy, tweedy, beer-drinking and jolly' – and other Inkling members included Charles Williams, Neville Coghill and J.R.R. Tolkien. It was here that Tolkien read aloud the first drafts of his fantasy saga *The Lord of the Rings*.

Lewis's mind began to wander. Perhaps one day he, like Morse, would merit some form of recognition? On the wall above their table he imagined a memorial plaque and inscribed upon it the words: 'Chief Inspector Morse, with his friend and colleague Sergeant Lewis, sat in this back room one Thursday, in order to solve...'

Investigating Oxfordshire

'How'd you figure out where they [the boots worn during the murderer] were?'

'Well, that's just it. I was loading the dishwasher, you know, humming a little tune, and boom, I just knew.'

SUE GRAFTON, *M IS FOR MURDER*

QUESTION: WHAT IS the connection between a dog-eared, Ambre Solaire-stained copy of *The Dead of Jericho* and seventy-five million people. Answer: Television.

Some time in the summer of 1985 Ted Childs, the controller of drama at Central Television, contacted producer Kenny McBain to ask if he had any ideas for a detective series. The BBC was screening a highly popular run of Agatha Christie adaptations and Childs thought his Birmingham-based company was missing out.

McBain had just the thing. 'I've been reading these novels by Colin Dexter,' the producer told his boss. 'They feature a detective and they're set in Oxford.'

While McBain arranged a meeting with Colin Dexter at his North Oxford home, Childs bought himself a set of the first six Morse novels. 'I've still got them somewhere,' he admits. 'It was summer so they're covered in Ambre Solaire because I read them in the garden.'

From the start, Childs and McBain wanted *Morse* to be something innovative and different – a decision that produced more than its share of sceptics. By the late 1980s, most television drama was being recorded on videotape. As the technical successor to film, it was cheaper and easier to use. *Morse*, from day one, would be shot on 16mm film to give it cinema-quality colour and depth.

Convincing Central's executives to accept their next suggestion was a little more difficult. Childs and McBain wanted each screen episode to run for sixty-five minutes, two hours including commercials. 'A lot of people were very reluctant to accept this innovation,' says Childs. 'The accepted belief at the time was that a television audience would not sit through a rather convoluted piece of detection for that length of time.'

---

over: The Woodstock Arms *was one of Morse's favourite pubs. 'The landlady rightly prided herself on a particularly fine pint of Morrell's Bitter'*

Almost eighteen months later, on Tuesday, 6 January 1987, British television viewers watched as a burgundy Mark II Jaguar drove on to the forecourt of a garage. The man at the wheel, looking slightly bored, was Chief Inspector Morse. Seconds later, thirteen million viewers let out a collective 'Ouch' as his pride and joy was rammed by a getaway car.

For those who enjoy facts and figures, that first episode – *The Dead of Jericho* – cost £1 million to make, or £500,000 per screen hour. By the final series twelve years later, the cost had doubled. For Carlton, it was a spectacular investment. British audiences quickly rose to an average eighteen million. *Morse* was sold to television companies from Angola to Zambia. At one time a worldwide survey estimated that no less than 750 million people regularly sat down to watch what can only be described as a very British detective at work.

By the summer of 1998 – just two months before his sixty-eighth birthday – Chief Inspector Morse retreated almost permanently to his music, his favourite wireless programmes and his North Oxford flat. Outside, millions waited for him to die. It was possibly the most trumpeted and anticipated departure in literary history. Morse, the thinking man's detective and everyone's working-class hero, was about to solve his last case. There was more bad news. After toying with all manner of send-offs for his hero, including retirement and marriage, Colin Dexter decided death was the 'only believable option'. There would be no second chances, no Reichenbach Falls for Morse. After years of heavy smoking and unhealthy living, he would succumb to a diabetic coma and slip away in hospital the next day, a final, whispered message to Sergeant Lewis on his lips.

But all this is premature. While Dexter may have decided *The Remorseful Day* was to be his thirteenth and final Morse novel, there is still a lot we don't know about his policeman hero.

In *The Making of Inspector Morse*, Mark Sanderson offers his own explanation:

> Morse is a sort of Philip Larkin figure, unlucky in love, swanning round the
> Oxford of the 1950s – where there is never a shortage of parking spaces –
> dreaming of books and beer. Morse and Lewis are the kind of people we can
> depend on and trust. In an age when corruption appears to be endemic to all
> levels of society their innate decency and passionate belief in justice strikes an
> emotional chord.

There is more to it than that. After all, Morse's reputation – his genius – came from solving the most brutal and savage of all crimes – murder. But before attempting to examine Morse's methods we must first trace his career.

In modern police ideology, Morse would have been flagged as a 'high flyer'. In 1955, at the suggestion of his dying father, Morse applied for and was accepted by the Royal

Berkshire Constabulary. His progress through the police ranks, alternating between uniformed and plain-clothes branches, was both predictable and rapid.

Twelve years later, as the five separate forces that policed the rural counties of Berkshire, Buckinghamshire and Oxfordshire and the urban populations of Reading and Oxford prepared for amalgamation, Morse was already a Detective Inspector. 'I missed the 1960s,' he once confessed to Sergeant Lewis. 'I was based at Windsor when the Rolling Stones played on Eel Pie Island.'

After serving as a Detective Inspector with the newly formed Thames Valley Constabulary – now Thames Valley Police – he arrived at the force's headquarters with a recent promotion to Chief Inspector and a reputation as a highly intelligent and equally efficient thief taker. The home the police authority had chosen for its headquarters was Kidlington on the banks of the River Cherwell and, with a population of more than 17,000, officially listed as England's largest village.

Today, passing motorists see only a ribbon development of 1930s houses, but tucked away is the heart of an ancient village. St Mary's Church was completed in 1220 on the site of a pre-Norman church. The impressive 175-foot spire was added in the fifteenth century. Other surviving buildings include a sixteenth-century farm, some large Georgian houses and Hampden House with its eighteenth-century pavilion and a recently rediscovered privy attributed to Vanbrugh, architect of Blenheim Palace.

Serving a population of 2.1 million people and covering the 2,200 square miles of Berkshire, Buckinghamshire and Oxfordshire, the Thames

Thames Valley Police – and Morse – are based at Kidlington, England's biggest village

Valley Police is the largest non-metropolitan force in the country. Each year it is also responsible for the safety of six million visitors who come, as the force's website states, 'in search of history, royalty and Inspector Morse'.

The three-storey, late 1960s office block from which Morse operated is, unlike in the novels, not a front-line police station. Its departments and facilities represent the support arm of any major police force: a radio-control room; an armoury; vehicle workshops; and civilian administrative staff. In reality, its appearance is not far removed from the images offered in the television stories.

When it came to filming the exterior shots of Morse's base, two different locations were used. The early TV episodes used a derelict Ministry of Defence laboratory in Harefield, now demolished to make way for a housing estate. Later filming was done at a shabby Territorial Army centre in Harrow, North London.

There are several errors of convenience in both the novels and the television adaptations. In the concluding pages of *Last Bus to Woodstock*, the Chief Inspector visits Sue Widdowson in 'cell number 1' of the police headquarters' north wing. In the TV story *Masonic Mysteries*, Morse is held in the Kidlington cells after being framed for murder by the arch-villain Hugo de Vries. In reality, there are no cells at Kidlington, the nearest custody suite is eight miles away.

Although the cases on which Morse and Lewis work are calendar correct – the first in 1975, the last in 1999 – the stage on which the pair roams and the methods they employ are firmly fixed in the mid-1960s. Colin Dexter has created a highly accurate and believable set while somehow managing to move the background in real time. Even allowing for his eccentric but efficient behaviour, and the obliging patronage of a Chief Constable, the days of a free-ranging Detective Chief Inspector are long gone.

The Thames Valley force has never used traditional 'murder squads' operating from its headquarters. Murders and serious crimes requiring little more than evidence gathering are always dealt with by CID officers from the local police area. More protracted inquiries are overseen by a senior investigating officer, usually a Detective Superintendent, and managed from an incident room near the crime scene by a Detective Inspector. Even then it would be rare for Kidlington officers to be involved.

After the discovery of a third body in *Service of All the Dead*, Morse is recalled from holiday and ordered to take over the case from the flu-ridden Chief Inspector Bell. Unusually, Morse and Lewis take up temporary residence in Bell's St Aldate's office.

The autonomous Oxford City Police of Dexter's novels, over whose patch the pair apparently function with impunity, appears to operate alongside but independently of the surrounding Thames Valley force, a relationship shared by the City of London and Metropolitan forces. At one time, Oxford was policed by an entirely separate force, which was funded by the city council. Today, it is one of Thames Valley's ten sub-divisions with a boundary almost exactly matching that of the city council.

Then there is the question of Morse's age. Colin Dexter has maintained that, like himself, his creation was born in Stamford, Lincolnshire, in the final days of September, 1930.

Throughout the early novels, Morse's age – rarely given – has progressed in line with his career. He is forty-five and already a Chief Inspector when he makes his first appearance in

Last Bus to Woodstock; he celebrates his fifty-first birthday shortly before *The Dead of Jericho* investigation; and in 1994 in *The Daughters of Cain*, he is threatened with demotion and, at the age of sixty-four, even considers retirement.

The fact that at the start of *The Remorseful Day* he is approaching his sixty-seventh birthday – more than eleven years past the obligatory pensionable age for the majority of police officers – and is still on the Thames Valley payroll appears only marginally exceptional considering Morse's obvious talent for solving murders. The force does allow its inspectors to continue working until they reach sixty-five, beyond at the discretion of the Chief Constable. It is a patronage Morse certainly enjoys.

What is frequently overlooked is Dexter's unintentional sleight-of-hand allowing him to 'clock' six years from the Chief Inspector's age.

'I've heard that sex can be very good for the over sixty-fives,' Morse informs his sergeant in *The Jewel That Was Ours*.

'Only ten years for you to go, then,' responds Lewis, establishing his boss's age as fifty-five.

With the action of the book set in 1991, and taken in sequence, Morse would in 'reality' already be in his sixty-first year. The error is easily explained. *The Jewel That Was Ours*, unlike the other twelve books, was novelised by Dexter from a television story line screened three years earlier as *The Wolvercote Tongue*. He developed the pre-script outline during 1985 – the year in which Morse celebrates his fifty-fifth birthday.

Morse's experience and expertise had elevated him far beyond the status of a simple detective. A regular speaker on 'Inner City Crime' at Metropolitan Police conferences, he also lectured at Kidlington on 'Homicide Procedures' to newly promoted CID officers.

> 'In the great majority of murder cases the identity of the accused is apparent
>   virtually from the start. You realise that? In about 40 per cent of such cases
>   he's arrested, almost immediately, at or very near the scene of the crime –
>   usually, and mercifully for the likes of you, Lewis, because he hasn't made
>   the slightest effort to escape. Now – let me get it right – in about 50 per cent
>   of cases the victim and the accused have had some prior relationship with
>   each other, often a very close relationship.'
> 'Interesting, Sir,' said Lewis as he turned off left just opposite the Thames
>   Valley Police HQ. 'You been giving another one of your lectures?'

It was the unravelling of those other percentages that Morse was good at, even if it did involve the occasional illegal act.

It was certainly not beyond Morse's resourcefulness to pressure a telephone inquiry through by claiming to be the Chief Constable; nor hastily to pocket a search warrant before a suspicious householder had time to read the benefits of a new police pension plan; nor, on several occasions, to investigate another officer's case. In *Death is Now My Neighbour*, Morse recruits reformed burglar Malcolm 'J.J.' Johnson to help him break into the Kidlington home of a murder suspect.

When Morse scented a solution, he could be ferocious to stop. 'He was here till way gone midnight,' recalls Constable Dickson during the *Last Bus to Woodstock* investigation. 'Got virtually everyone in the building jumping about for him. I reckon every phone on the premises was red hot. God, he can work when he wants to.' Unfortunately, as Lewis knew from experience, while Morse was galloping ahead of the pack, he too often found himself on the wrong racecourse.

In *Last Seen Wearing*, Sergeant Lewis reflects on his second major case with an officer whom many within the Thames Valley Police – from the Chief Constable down – considered a genius.

> The real trouble was that he [Morse] always had to find a complex solution to everything, and Lewis had enough experience of police work to know that criminal activity owed its origins to simple, cheap, and sordid motives, and that few of the criminals themselves had sufficiently intelligent or tortuous minds to devise the cunning stratagems that Morse was wont to attribute to them. In Morse's mind the simple facts of any case seemed somewhere along the line to get fitted out with hooks and eyes which rendered the possibility of infinite associations and combinations. What the great man couldn't do, for all his gifts, was put a couple of simple facts together and come up with something obvious.

Another thing Morse could not do was apologise for his outbursts of ill-timed intolerance and ill-tempered frustration, at least, not with any good grace or conviction. When an apology did come, as in *The Dead of Jericho*, it was left to Lewis to gauge the depth of his boss's sincerity: 'We're a team, we are – you realise that, don't you? You and me, when we work together – Christ! We're bloody near invincible!'

The only piece of career advice Lewis received from his father – and only partly appropriate at times like these – was that he 'should always keep his mouth mostly shut and his bowels always open'. Whether Lewis senior survived long enough to appreciate the fruits of his paternal counsel is not known, nor do we know much of his son's early life.

But where do we start? The popular and affable Sergeant Lewis of the television stories is not the Lewis of the early books. 'When I first wrote him, he was the same age as me,' explains Colin Dexter, 'and that was roughly the same age as Morse. Certainly in the first book, I thought he was a grandfather.'

Lewis, like his superior's car, has been transformed by the pressure of popularity. In *Last Bus to Woodstock*, Lewis is middle-aged and Morse is content to drive a classic Lancia. By the time the first *Morse* episode was screened, Lewis had lost fifteen to twenty years, and as many pounds, and Morse had swapped his Lancia for a Mark II Jaguar.

By the time Dexter came to write the second half of his Morse series, he too was imagining Lewis as a reflection of the sergeant's television persona, and his publishers had reprinted and reissued the early novels with a sneaky change of vehicle. So what do we know of this re-invented Lewis?

Born in Newcastle-upon-Tyne during the early years of the Second World War, the young Robert Lewis – Robbie to his family and friends – was determined not to be seduced by the security of an engineering apprenticeship into a job offering a soulless future. He did take a job with one of Tyneside's largest employers, but only because they would allow him time off to attend day-release courses.

At eighteen, three years after leaving school, Lewis was called up for national service. His abilities in the ring were soon spotted and he spent the better part of his two years in the army upholding his unit's reputation at regimental and inter-service boxing tournaments as its most 'useful light-middleweight'. The police force, as Lewis readily admitted, seemed a natural progression.

Lewis never returned to the north-east. Like Morse, the police force he originally joined was one of the four that merged to form the Thames Valley Constabulary. By 1971, Lewis had earned his sergeant's stripes and a permanent place in the Criminal Investigation Department.

On Wednesday, 29 September 1975, Lewis was on duty at the force's Kidlington headquarters when the telephone rang. The manager of the Black Prince at Woodstock wanted to report the discovery of a woman's body in the pub's car park. Within fifteen minutes Lewis was conferring with a Chief Inspector who, by reputation, was already a force legend.

Morse, too, was impressed by the thick-set, slightly awkward-looking man.

> 'Shall I get you some more help, Sergeant?'
> 'I think the two of us can manage, Sir.'
> 'Good. Let's get started.'

Their early collaboration in *Last Bus to Woodstock* cements a classic twenty-four-year partnership in British crime fiction. 'As the great detective's foil and sidekick, Lewis is essentially a straight man,' explains Christopher Bird in his *World of Inspector Morse*. 'Lewis is a counterpart who on the one hand is dull enough to allow the other's genius to shine

out, and on the other possesses enough common sense and traditional wisdom to call the divinely inspired superman back to reality.'

During the many, many hours he had spent in Morse's company on the several murder cases that had fallen within their sphere of duty, there had been frequent occasions when Lewis had wished him in hell. But there were infinitely worthwhile compensations – were there not? – in being linked with a man of Morse's almost mythical methodology. For all his superior's irascibility, crudity, and self-indulgence Lewis had taken enormous pride – yes, *pride* – in his friendship with the man whom almost all the other members of the Thames Valley Constabulary had now come to regard as a towering, if somewhat eccentric, genius. And in the minds of many the phenomenon of Morse was directly associated with *himself* – yes, with *Lewis*! They spoke of Morse and Lewis almost in the same vein as they spoke of Gilbert and Sullivan, or Moody and Sank, or Lennon and McCartney.

Over the years and through the dozen or so murder cases, Lewis not only becomes an honest and trusted friend but, in many ways, the bachelor Morse's surrogate 'wife'. He encourages his partner and frustrates him – 'You'll never get on, Lewis, until you have mastered your subjunctives' – just as any spouse married to a man of

Born within sight of the Tyne, Lewis rejected Newcastle's traditional industries for a career in the police force

Morse's intellect would. And, in the later years, when Morse's drinking habits are having such a debilitating effect on his health, Lewis turns to concerned nagging.

But Lewis, whose only faults appear to be an addiction to fried egg and chips and a passion for fast driving, already has a wife and two children, Lyn and Ken.

Born in the Rhondda Valley, Valerie Lewis is a dedicated mother and an exceptionally perceptive wife. Not only is she apparently happy to fashion her own existence around the unusual hours and demands of her husband's job – and his even more trying boss – but, like her husband, she shares a thankful admiration for Morse. She would never admit it to her husband, but whenever the two detectives are working together, a 'curious contentment' shows itself in Lewis's eyes.

Irritated by Morse's out-of-hours telephone calls and her husband's disrupted days off, Valerie Lewis is more than happy to cook an extra serving of egg and chips or watch Morse relax – just once – with a beer after Sunday lunch. It may be Lewis who calls on a sick Morse to ensure he takes his medicine, but it is Valerie who ensures her husband arrives with a clean pair of pyjamas.

There is only one other man whom Morse respects enough to call a friend – and over whose death he weeps. Maximilian Theodore Siegfried de Bryn – a man equally intent on concealing his Christian names – makes his first anonymous appearance in *Last Seen Wearing*.

> 'Well?' asked Morse.
> 'Difficult to say. Anywhere from sixteen to twenty
>   hours.'
> 'Can you pin it down any closer?'
> 'No.'

In the hump-backed, hard-drinking, police-hating pathologist, Morse had at last found someone brave enough to trade verbal punches and wise enough to share his own sense of melancholy. For his own part, there was only one policeman for whom Max would allow himself a sliver of admiration, and that was because Morse, over a few beers, had informed the scientist he had a 'most profound contempt for the timid twaddle' uttered by the majority of pathologists.

The contrast between the two men would have struck any observer that morning. The stout, hump-backed surgeon – circumspect, but perky and confident; Morse – looking distinctly weary, his jowls semi-shaven by an electric razor that had seemingly passed peak efficiency, and yet somehow, somewhere underneath, a man on the side of the angels.

Turned on since boyhood by the sight of blood, Max was a world authority on venereal disease. His office and mortuary are somewhere inside the Sir William Dunn School of Pathology on South Parks Road, where numerous scenes for the television episodes have been shot. An experimental department within Oxford University, the Dunn School, which moved into its purpose-built laboratory in 1926, is most famous for its pre-war pioneering work on penicillin.

In *The Way Through the Woods*, Morse is working in his Kidlington office when news reaches the police headquarters of Max's death. It was only the third time Morse had wept for a fellow human being.

The previous afternoon, Morse had visited the semi-conscious police surgeon in the coronary care unit at the John Radcliffe Hospital. 'I'll bring us a bottle of malt in the morning, Max, and we'll have a wee drop together, my old friend. So keep a hold on things – please keep a hold on things!... Just for me!'

Later that morning, Morse is called at the Dunn School and meets Max's successor, Dr Laura Hobson. As they sit lamenting Max's death, Morse quotes a line from *Bleak House*: 'The cart is shaken all to pieces, and the rugged road is at its end.'

It is the nature of the television medium to gobble up locations almost as voraciously as it consumes actors. When you condense a 365-page novel into sixty-five minutes of screen time, something has to go. The first victim is invariably Colin Dexter's mischievous sense of history.

In *The Way Through the Woods*, Morse takes over the 'Swedish maiden affair'. The next morning he and Lewis drive out to Wytham Woods to begin their own inquiries.

The novel The Way Through The Woods *and the television episode* The Secret of Bay 5B *both feature Wytham Woods*

> Many Oxonians know 'Wytham' as the village on the way to the woods. But
> Morse knew the spot as the village, situated on the edge of the wood, which
> housed the White Hart Inn; and he pointed lovingly to the hostelry as Lewis
> drove the pair of them to their meeting with the head forester.
> 'Did you know,' asked Morse (consulting his leaflet) 'that in the parish of
> Wytham, a large part of it covered with woods, the ground rises from the
> banks of the Thames – or 'Isis' – to a height of 539ft at Wytham Hill, the
> central point of the ancient parish?'
> 'No, Sir,' replied Lewis, turning right just after the pub into a stretch of
> progressively narrowing roadway that was very soon marked by the sign
> 'Private Property: University of Oxford'.

The Old English word for a sharp bend in a road or river is 'wiht'. When an estate or manor is found nearby, the suffix 'ham' was added. So it was that a small group of thatched, stone cottages north west of Oxford came to be known as Wytham. The spelling may have evolved, but the River Thames still flows around a sharp bow nearby and a vast tract of land owned by Abingdon Abbey can be traced back as far as AD 955 and the reign of King Eadwig.

By the twelfth century, the church estate had been leased to the de Wytham family – pronounced locally as 'Whitem' – and not only included the village but several hundred acres of woodland. Today, the 960 acres of Wytham Woods are closed to the public. Designated a Site of Special Scientific Interest, the ancient forest is maintained as a wildlife and plant sanctuary and research resource.

The Way Through the Woods is dedicated to Brian Bedwell. It was after chatting to Bedwell, a police sergeant, in an Oxford public house that Colin Dexter was motivated to write his tenth Morse mystery.

During the 1980s, *The Times* anonymously received a succession of chess notations and crude maps claiming to indicate where the body of a murder victim was buried. The new 'evidence' sparked weeks of correspondence from both lay readers and experts, but an exact location was never pinpointed. After several abortive searches by the police, it was decided the original letters were nothing more than an elaborate hoax.

In the novel, Thames Valley police receive a five-stanza poem allegedly written by 'A. Austin (1835–87)' and purporting to solve the disappearance in Oxford of the Scandinavian tourist, Karin Eriksson. The verses are studied by *The Times* literary correspondent Howard Philippson before publication and, like the original case, raise a flurry of fanciful solutions. At the time, Philippson's real-life counterpart on the newspaper was Philip Howard.

*Woodstock: Where 'the strong grey houses have witnessed
older times and could tell their older tales'*

The verses are first published in *The Times* while Morse is on holiday in Lyme Regis and it is not long before his own contributions to the debate, published under the name 'Lionel Regis', begin to appear. A body is eventually unearthed in Wytham Woods, but it is far from what Morse expected.

For the dedicated Morse fan, the city of Oxford has few rivals. But the historic town of Woodstock, and the nearby Blenheim Palace estate, play a no less impressive, although smaller, part in two Morse novels – *Last Bus to Woodstock* and *The Way Through the Woods*. In the early pages of *Last Bus to Woodstock*, Colin Dexter describes the drive to the town:

> The journey from Oxford to Woodstock is quietly attractive. Broad grass verges afford a pleasing sense of spaciousness, and at the village of Yarnton, after a couple of miles, a dual carriageway, with three-lined central reservation, finally sweeps the accelerating traffic past the airport and away from its earlier paralysis. For a mile immediately before Woodstock, on the left-hand side a grey stone wall marks the eastern boundary of the extensive and beautiful grounds of Blenheim Palace, the mighty mansion built by good Queen Anne for her brilliant general, John Churchill, 1st Duke of Marlborough. High and imposing wrought-iron gates mark the main entrance to the palace drive, and hither flock the tourists in the summer season to walk amidst the dignified splendour of the great rooms, to stand before the vast Flemish tapestries of Malplaquet and Oudenarde, and to see the room in which was born that later scion of the Churchill line, the great Sir Winston himself, now lying in the once-peaceful churchyard of nearby Bladon village.

According to the *Oxford Dictionary of English Place Names*, the word Woodstock means 'place in the woods' and that, for several centuries, is exactly what it was – a place in the vast rambling forest that stretched from the Cotswolds to London, where royalty and its entourage hunted and relaxed.

Much of old Woodstock still survives:

> The strong grey houses which line the main street have witnessed older times and could tell their older tales, though now the majority are sprucely converted into gift, antique and souvenir shops – and inns. There was always, it appears, a goodly choice of hostelries, and several of the hotels and inns now clustered snugly along the streets can boast not only an ancient lineage but also a cluster of black AA stars on their bright yellow signs.

Woodstock: the small Oxfordshire market town where Morse and Lewis first worked together in Last Bus to Woodstock

over: A condition of the nation's gift to John Churchill was that Blenheim should remain a symbol of Britain's supremacy. Today the 2,700-acre estate is one of Britain's top visitor attractions

But, as so often happens, popular fiction has a far greater sway on marketing and tourism than recorded history.

The Black Prince public house, where the body of Sylvia Kaye was found in the car park and where Morse and Sergeant Lewis collaborate for the first time in *Last Bus to Woodstock*, was a Colin Dexter invention inspired by the 1330 birth of Edward, the Black Prince, in Woodstock. During filming for the 1988 television adaptation, the town's fifteenth-century Marlborough Arms – redressed and renamed the Fox and Castle – was used as a stand-in. Not long after the story was screened, one of the town's other pubs changed its name to the Black Prince – to cash in on the Morse connection.

At the far end of Park Street, where the poet Geoffrey Chaucer lived for several years and where his home still stands, is an impressive arch which marks the entrance to the 2,700-acre Blenheim estate. For Morse and Lewis, the estate produces a vital clue and an unexpected death.

In *The Way Through the Woods*, George Daley, one of the estate's garden centre workers, finds a rucksack on the A44 near Woodstock. It belonged to the missing Swedish student Karin Eriksson. Under pressure from Morse, he finally admits his son developed a roll of film from the victim's camera, concealing vital evidence. In a surprising twist to the plot, Daley is later murdered and his body dumped on the Blenheim estate.

Today, Blenheim Palace arguably owes its survival and upkeep to the thousands of tourists who visit the estate each year, but its existence and splendour are due to an obscure and long-forgotten war.

In August 1704, John Churchill, the Duke of Marlborough, inflicted a crushing defeat on the French army marching on Vienna near the Bavarian village of Blenheim. His victory significantly changed the balance of power in the War of the

---

Blenheim Palace provides an impressive and fatal attraction in
Last Bus to Woodstock *and* The Way Through The Woods

Spanish Succession, and as a token of the nation's gratitude Queen Anne presented him with Woodstock Manor.

A condition of the endowment was that it was to be no mere private house, but a national symbol of Britain's supremacy. Sir John Vanbrugh, whose designs for Castle Howard were greatly admired by Churchill, was commissioned to design and build the new Blenheim Palace.

The project never ran smoothly. Vanbrugh incessantly complained because he was forced to live in the semi-derelict old manor house, still bearing the scars of a Civil War bombardment, to oversee the building work. Funds ran out and Parliament wrangled over the cost. The animosity between the Duke and his architect became so bitter that Vanbrugh never saw the completed building. When he arrived unannounced in 1725, the Duchess ordered the gates to be locked and Vanbrugh turned away.

Even as a finished 'monument to commemorate a military victory and to glorify the Queen', Blenheim attracted more than its share of controversy. Horace Walpole described the palace's bizarre skyline as 'execrable' and the ever practical Alexander Pope quipped "tis very fine; but where d'ye sleep and where d'ye dine?'

One of the last deaths Morse would investigate was in the town of Burford

Despite its size and obvious discomforts, Blenheim served as a home for successive Dukes; the present owner is the eleventh. Sir Winston Churchill was born in the palace in 1874 and, after a distinguished career as a politician, writer and war leader, was buried in a simple grave in the parish church of Bladon on the southern edge of the estate.

Every episode of *Morse* was a magic blend of the real and imagined. Locations were chosen because they were geographically correct or conformed to the scriptwriter's vision. When the real thing proved impractical, a look-alike substitute was found. The car park of an 'Oxford' shop could, in reality, be anywhere in the Home Counties.

This is hardly encouraging for anyone determined to discover *Inspector Morse Country*, but what if Colin Dexter's own locations are missing from a map of Oxfordshire? It is, in fact, rare for Dexter to rely entirely on fictional locations – there is always a clue.

The murder scene in *The Silent World of Nicholas Quinn* is the Foreign Examinations Syndicate based in 'one of those Victorian streets in North Oxford which link the Woodstock and Banbury roads'. Much of the novel's action takes place in the syndicate's Chaucer Road headquarters, but neither the Syndicate – which has its inspiration in the Oxford Delegacy of Local Examinations – nor Chaucer Road exist; nor does Pinewood Close, Kidlington, where Quinn lives and where his body is discovered.

In Morse's third investigation, the eponymous Quinn is appointed to the examination body's graduate staff despite misgivings about his profound deafness. His post is secured, and his death sealed, by his lip-reading skills. It is familiar ground for Dexter who, despite his own hearing loss, worked for many years for an Oxford public examinations board.

As a venue for a two-day conference organised by the Foreign Examinations Syndicate, Dexter invents the luxury Sheridan Hotel on St Giles'.

In *The Remorseful Day*, the author, unusually by this time, chooses to invent a location for Morse's final investigation. Frank Harrison, summoned by a mysterious telephone call, arrives at Oxford railway station late one night in the summer of 1997 and travels the ten miles to his home in the Cotswold village of Lower Swinstead in a taxi. Inside his £350,000 listed Georgian house the banker discovers the battered body of his wife, Yvonne. The village – and its only public house, the Maiden's Arms – do not exist, unlike the town of Burford, used in the same novel, where Patricia Bayley retired with her husband in the mid-1990s. Two months later, her husband, a distinguished anthropologist from University College, collapsed and died.

By 1997, the windows and paintwork of their 'dream cottage' in Burford's Sheep Street were showing signs of wear and Mrs Bayley scanned the *Yellow Pages* for a suitable contractor. She found and contacted 'J. Barron, Builder and Decorator' of Lower Swinstead who, as promised, duly arrived at 7.30 a.m. on Monday, 3 August to start work. Within minutes, he was dead – *The Remorseful Day*'s fourth victim.

Burford – the real Burford – was on the edge of Morse's jurisdiction. A sleepy town of few permanent residents and many peripatetic tourists, it had, over the past 700 years been a market town, a centre for cloth manufacture, a notable leather town, a racing centre second only to Newmarket until the last century, and a town of coaches and inns.

> Twenty miles west of Oxford, twenty miles east of Cheltenham, lies the little Cotswold town of Burford. It owes its architectural attractiveness to the wealth of the wool merchants in the fifteenth and sixteenth centuries; and up until the end of the eighteenth century the small community there continued to thrive, especially the coaching inns which regularly served the E-W travel. But the town was no longer expanding, with the final blow delivered in 1812, when the main London road, which crossed the High Street (the present day Sheep Street and Witney Street), was rerouted to the southern side of the town (the present day A40). But Burford remains an enchanting place, as summer tourists will happily testify as they turn off at the A40 roundabout. Picturesque tea shops, craft shops, public houses – all built in the locally quarried, pale-honey-coloured limestone – line the steeply curving sweep of the High Street that leads to the bridge at the bottom of the hill, under which runs the River Windrush, with all the birds and the bright meadows and cornfields around Oxfordshire.

There is still hope. On the way into the town, Morse spotted the strangely angular lines and the green window canopies of the Cotswold Gateway Hotel. 'Why don't we sit back and look at what we've got,' said Morse, sipping from his pint of cask-conditioned ale. 'Let's look at the evidence.'

Morse Further Afield

THERE IS A MODERN philosopher who expounded the theory that life is like driving a car. Occasionally you need to look in the rear-view mirror to see where you have come from, to make sense of your own history and to understand where you are going. Of course, if you spend all your time looking back, you are bound to crash. There is another type of driver who is so afraid of his past, so scared of what it has turned him into, that he refuses to use his mirror at all – until something long out of sight and memory threatens to overtake and change his world once more.

'I can't imagine you young, Morse,' comments Superintendent Strange in *Cherubim and Seraphim*. In fact, we know so little of Morse's early life, and he scatters his childhood tidbits so sparsely, that it is soon obvious into which profile he falls.

When his stepmother was prescribed a drug that revived not only her memory but her bitter hatred for Morse, and his half-sister's teenaged daughter died from a drug-related suicide, the Chief Inspector's world was suddenly under threat. For the first time since leaving his Lincolnshire birthplace, Morse found himself blinded by the glare of his deliberately suppressed memories.

But it is not just the past that stalked Morse. He was equally haunted by the future. The adult Morse had inherited a morbid fear of progress and change. 'Morse was capable of being disproportionately upset by a good many things,' explains Dexter. 'The sight of death, beautiful women and litter.'

Travel, another kind of change, was only ever tackled on Morse's terms – or under orders. Holidays, like his pursuit of women, were always organised and with a purpose. The journey may be interesting and instructive, but who could tell what he might find or unleash on his arrival.

Asked by an inquisitive prostitute why he had never married, Morse replied, 'I was always too choosy, too hesitant, too lazy, or too busy.' Perhaps his hesitation was rooted not so much in the fact that he would have been forced to relinquish his independence, but more that he would have been cornered into giving up the gentler, pre-technology existence he cherished.

At home in his North Oxford flat, he refused to use or own a computer, preferring to write his reports and letters by hand. He possessed a television but preferred the wireless and was a devoted fan of 'The Archers'. Although he owned a CD player (for quality of sound), he still bought 'records' and played them on his 'stereo', and he insisted on driving a 'pre-electrics' car. He paid little attention to modern appliances in the kitchen, or the food they produced. One day, for no obvious reason, he was tempted to buy himself a microwave oven. It departed after they 'fought'.

Whether he would have fought with a wife is something only Morse and his creator can answer but it is hard to imagine Morse allowing himself to be badgered by the equivalent of Rumpole's 'she who must be obeyed' or Arthur Daley's 'her indoors'.

So where does all this inner conflict originate? 'Unless a writer of detective fiction is a genius of invention,' Colin Dexter once admitted, 'there is almost inevitably going to be an element of semi-autobiography.' Disengaging Dexter from his hero is a difficult but fascinating task.

The story starts almost ninety miles north of Oxford in the picturesque Lincolnshire market town of Stamford. It was here that Morse, like his creator, was born and educated.

Only once in thirteen novels and seven short stories does Morse revisit his birthplace. It's not that he harbours any fear of returning or animosity towards Stamford; for the most part he enjoyed his schooldays and, until his parents separated, he was a happy and contented child. It is simply that Morse has no reason to return.

Both his parents are dead and we never learn the fate of his half-sister, Joyce. Living somewhere near Berwick in Northumberland was an aunt. Looking down on Stamford from the top of Easton Hill in the 1980s, Morse realised the 'grey stone buildings matching the spires and towers' had changed little in almost three decades.

Morse rarely spoke while in a car. If he was driving he would listen to classical music. If Sergeant Lewis was driving, he would sink 'silent and morose' into his own thoughts. Perhaps, while Lewis drove those final miles in *Service of All the Dead*, Morse was remembering his Stamford childhood.

Nineteen-thirty was a good year for working-class heroes – the British airwoman Amy Johnson completed a series of record-breaking flights; at fifty-two, Wilfred Rhodes became the oldest man to play in a Test match, against the West Indies; the jockey Gordon Richards rode his twelfth consecutive winner in three days; and George Bernard Shaw refused the offer of a peerage. It was also a good year for one working-class couple who were eagerly anticipating the birth of their first child.

Mr Morse was a handsome, strong-willed man who, when he wasn't driving his taxi around the streets of Stamford, was enthusiastically following his own particular hero. His wife was a 'gentle soul' whose Quaker parents instilled in her the righteousness of hard work and the tolerance to accept her husband's passionate lectures on Captain James Cook.

Cook, as Mrs Morse knew only too well, was an eighteenth-century navigator and explorer, credited with mapping much of eastern Australia and discovering Antarctica and several Pacific islands including Hawaii. His ship was HMS *Endeavour*.

In the final week of September 1930, Mrs Morse gave birth to a son. It was no surprise, least of all to the recovering mother and the family's near relatives, that her husband should announce that the boy should be christened and registered as Endeavour Morse – an eccentricity his son would spend the rest of his life attempting to conceal.

No one knows exactly when the Morses moved to Stamford. The name has its roots among the farmers and agricultural workers of Oxfordshire. It may well be that the historic link between Oxford and Lincolnshire – which surfaces more than once in Morse's own life – is responsible for his ancestors move north.

Stamford was a quiet, gentle place in which to grow up. A small Lincolnshire town on the east coast

Captain James Cook
after whose ship Morse was named

of England, for centuries Stamford has attracted a long and literary line of admirers. The poet laureate Sir John Betjeman claimed Stamford was 'England's most attractive town'. Celia Fiennes, the late seventeenth-century traveller, described it as 'fine a built town all of stone as may be seen'. The novelist Sir Walter Scott apparently admired the view up to St Mary's Church, claiming it was the finest sight on the road between London and Edinburgh.

Lady Wedgewood, writing in 1936, said: 'Among stone-built towns there may be some that equal, none I think that surpassed, Stamford.' A few years earlier, Sir Nikolaus Pevsner, the architectural historian, recorded: 'The climax [of Lincolnshire] in terms of historical as well as architectural significance, is…the town of Stamford, the English country and market town *par excellence.'*

The most fulsome praise comes from W.G. Hoskins. 'If there is a more beautiful town in the whole of England I have yet to see it,' said the 1950s' historian. 'The view of Stamford from the water meadows on a fine June evening, about a quarter to half mile upstream, is one of the finest sights that England has to show. The Western sunlight catches the grey limestone walls and turns them to gold. It falls on towers and spires and flowing water, on the warm brown roofs of Collyweston slates, and on the dark mass of the Burghley woods behind.'

The history of Stamford stretches back far longer than the existence of the Great North Road beside which it now stands. Stamford first came into prominence in the ninth and tenth centuries when it was one of the five towns controlling the borough's Danelaw, a legal form of government originally imported by the Vikings from Denmark.

Under the Normans, the town became a thriving centre for the wool trade. One of its more famous products, also of Danish descent, was a woven cloth called 'haberget' – a twill fabric with a lozenge pattern.

Times were good. The town prospered because of its excellent communication routes, north and south by road and via the River Welland to the North Sea. By the thirteenth century, Stamford was one of the ten largest towns in England, with a castle, fourteen churches, two monastic institutions and four friaries. It was so important parliaments met there.

When England's wool trade moved towards the flat open countryside of East Anglia, Stamford and its townsfolk suffered. Two centuries of decline and stagnation followed, but the market town never lost its place in national affairs. Stamford-born William Cecil was appointed Secretary of State to Elizabeth I and built a palatial mansion just outside the town for his mother. Burghley House survives as one of the crowning glories of the Tudor age.

The town survived the Civil War relatively unscathed, despite Oliver Cromwell's siege of Burghley House and a visit by the fugitive King Charles in May 1646.

'Among stone-built towns there may be some that equal,
none I think that surpassed, Stamford'

After the restoration of 1660, improvements to the Great North Road once again put Stamford on the map as a transport and trade centre. A canal was built, reopening the River Welland's access to the sea. Anyone heading north from London passed through Stamford and the coaching trade elevated its old medieval inns into essential and nationally known hostelries.

By the second quarter of the ninteenth century, England was being criss-crossed by a new and faster highway. Now it was possible to transport people and goods from the capital to the north of England and Scotland cheaper than ever before. But the business moguls and engineers who sat down to plan Britain's expanding railways failed to draw a line on the map connecting Stamford with the rest of the network. Investment and industry passed the town by, fossilising the traditional, almost feudal, relationship between the town families and the rural landowning dynasties so that in the pre-war years of Morse's childhood, Stamford had changed little for almost a century.

To a nine-year-old boy, the Second World War brought a cascade of new sights and smells and sounds. By 1939, knots of young men in pale-blue uniforms were a familiar part of Morse's life. Overhead, low-flying bombers rattled the windows of Stamford's stone-built

Stamford where Morse was born in the final week of September, 1930 and where his father earned a living driving a taxi

over: Stamford Grammar School where Morse learned to enjoy the strict regime and developed a love of Greek

houses. Lincolnshire was the home of the Royal Air Force and the RAF was gearing up for war.

During the first winter of war, other young men arrived whose language Morse could not understand. First it was the Poles, then the Czechs and then, the following summer, the Free French. All of them, for as long as they were around, somehow managed to merge into the fabric of daily life. In 1943, it was Stamford that was forced to change.

To the unprepared and unsuspecting population, the arrival of the American Air Force was a noisy, blustering, back-slapping shock. For the rest of the town, it meant a sudden and much welcome flush of new money. For Morse's school friends – at least those with a spare bedroom or attic – it meant a ready supply of chewing gum and chocolate.

Even during the early years of war, the Morse household was still a calm and happy place. The drift from 'idyllic bliss to idiotic bickering' had not yet begun and the boy it produced still felt secure and eager to please. One afternoon, Morse came home from school with a letter announcing that he had earned himself a scholarship to the town's prestigious grammar school.

Stamford Grammar School was as physically imposing as its reputation for 'quiet success' was on the upper-middle class families of Britain. Overlooking the Great North Road just east of the town, and surrounded by acres of playing fields, it was, to the majority of parents preoccupied with conflict, a sanctum of relative safety in which to deposit their sons.

As Morse soon discovered, however, life within the limestone walls could be as unwelcoming as the chilly classrooms. Scholarship boys were tolerated by the masters and received with open hostility by the boarders. There was also a constant and brutal rivalry between the day boys, including Morse, and the boarders, most of whose fathers were either independently wealthy or of sufficient military rank to afford the annual fee.

Morse found few friends among the other day boys. The fact that he had earned his place on intelligence and merit won him little acceptance among the sons of local businessmen and land-owning farmers who, like their fathers, viewed a taxi driver as little more than a paid servant.

Paradoxically, Morse found the strict and unsympathetic regime strangely comforting. Education at Stamford Grammar was a six-day-a-week experience. The school survived on two uncompromising lores – learning and discipline.

There were few evenings when Morse did not have two, sometimes three, hours' homework, and Saturday school was followed by an afternoon's compulsory sports. Out of hours and out of school, posses of prefects scoured the town for younger pupils breaking curfew or flouting the jacket-and-tie dress code.

Each and every lesson at Stamford was devoted to the art of learning. It was a hard and painful process – for which Morse was later grateful – executed by a series of middle-aged, pedantic teachers who were only too willing to penalise lapses in grammar or punctuation or spelling with vicious glee.

A day or so after his induction at grammar school, Morse was given the option of entering the Greek, German or geography stream. He opted for Greek, a decision for which he would remain eternally grateful, and was soon enjoying his daily tussle with the paradigms of Greek grammar.

His knowledge of geography remained 'fatally flawed' and limited to what he learned by rote at junior school. As an adult, he was still able to name the capital cities of all the American states with the exception of South Dakota – useful for crosswords, but with little practical purpose. One of his favourite lessons was history and although all he could remember later was the workings of pioneer seed-drills and eighteenth-century agricultural trivia, he did manage a credit in his school certificate.

A smattering of schoolboy German and French somehow buried themselves in an alcove of Morse's brain, to be taken out occasionally, dusted off, used and derisively dismissed – 'He had always felt that a language which sanctioned the pronunciation of *donne*, *donnes* and *donnent* without the slightest differentiation could hardly deserve to be taken seriously.'

At school, Morse was a plodder. Never a quick thinker or reader, a burden he suffered for the rest of his life, the answers to examination questions always came slowly. He took his scholarship exam seated next to a boy renowned for his 'vacuous imbecility', and he remembered how his neighbour had solved the tenth anagram while he was still puzzling over the third.

About this time, Mr and Mrs Morse took their son to a music hall. One act involved nothing more than a woman dancing in front of a large mirror – 'She wasn't a particularly nimble-bodied thing, and yet the audience had seemed enthralled by her performance.' And then the reality struck him. There was not one woman but two, each mirroring the other's gestures.

With the war over, he could once again spend the school holidays wandering the 'Gipsy' meadows or swim in the river or drift through the beast-filled pens of Stamford's twice weekly market. In March each year, he would stand at the end of Broad Street and watch as the procession of brightly painted caravans and lorries arrived for the Mid-Lent Fair. But Stamford, like the atmosphere at home, was changing.

As a self-employed taxi driver, his father worked irregular hours. His absences from home grew longer and longer and Morse – he could never remember exactly how or when – was suddenly aware that his parents' marriage was over. After years of keeping his affair secret, Morse's father was leaving home to live with his lover.

Mrs Morse was a 'loving and kind' woman devoted to her son, and her betrayal by his father was something Morse would never forgive nor forget. But whatever his father's marital misdemeanours, Morse continued to love both his parents. 'Especially my father,' he admitted more than forty years after the taxi driver's death. 'He drank and gambled far too much, but I loved him. He knew nothing really – except two things. He could recite all of *Macaulay's Lays of Ancient Rome* by heart, and he'd read everything ever written about his greatest hero in life, Captain Cook – "Captain James Cook, 1728 to 1779", as he always used to call him.'

Morse continued to live with his mother, but the strain and the bitterness of the separation and divorce eventually took its toll. In the autumn after her son's fourteenth birthday, Mrs Morse's health began to deteriorate. News of her former husband's marriage to his 'fancy woman' and the birth, soon after, of a child of their own did not help. Within a year, Mrs Morse was dead and her son moved in, downcast and unhappy, with his father and stepmother and baby half-sister, Joyce.

Late in October 1948, the postman delivered a brown manilla envelope to Morse's home. It was time, the War Office decided, for him to start his national service. Two weeks later he reported to a local drill hall for his medical.

In December, and while Morse was still attending Stamford Grammar School, a second printed letter arrived informing the eighteen-year-old he was physically fit and that he would be drafted into the Royal Signals Regiment. With the letter was his first day's pay of five shillings and a list of personal effects he was expected to bring with him – a yellow duster, boot polish, a tin of Brasso.

The money was also expected to pay for a pre-enlistment haircut. With Christmas and New Year over, Morse visited a town-centre barber shop to have his regulation school short back and sides trimmed still shorter.

Early in January 1949, Morse caught the train north. At Northallerton in Yorkshire, an army truck was waiting to take

Haarlem: murder almost took Morse to Holland's Oxford

the latest batch of national-service recruits to Catterick Camp for twelve weeks' basic training. Eighteen months later, Morse was back in Stamford with several hundred pounds in his Post Office savings account and a mature taste for beer.

All this Morse keeps to himself. Only once, in the short story *The Carpet-Bagger*, does Morse hint at his roots, and then so obscurely he might have picked up the same information from his favoured trivia source – the back of a matchbox. When a fellow officer questions why a thief, Samuel Lambert, should be nicknamed 'Danny', Morse offers an answer. 'Might be someone from Stamford in Lincolnshire,' he said. 'Lamberts there often get called Danny, after Daniel Lambert – fellow who weighed fifty-two odd stone – still in *The Guinness Book of Records*.'

We only learn the details of his childhood when his creator cares to share them. In the foreword to Christopher Bird's *The World of Inspector Morse*, Dexter adds a little depth and colour to the outline of Morse's life:

> At school he was more sensitive to the arts than most of his classmates. In particular, Housman and Wagner have remained his greatest heroes (as they have mine). His temperament is melancholy, though far from gloomy. I suspect that as a pupil he was not overmuch amused by Shakespearean comedy but was strangely moved by the tragedies. In the sixth form he first learned (like me) about those 'tears shed for things', and knew that Virgil would be a lifelong companion. Like his beloved Hardy, he is probably more of a pejorist than a true pessimist. Yet he can see little hope for the future of the planet, believing as he does that human beings have a stronger predisposition towards evil than towards good.

Whatever his negative preoccupations, Morse had, since childhood, harboured an intense dislike of sport and holidays. Those twin obsessions were reinforced by his forced and unappreciated introduction to foreign travel.

In the television episode *The Settling of the Sun*, we learn that he was stationed in southern Germany during his national service. From its brief mention in *Service of All the Dead*, it is obvious his eight-week secondment to a West African police force in the autumn of 1976 was not one of his most enjoyable experiences. The African climate, like the political temperature, was prickly and unforgiving and Morse soon came to resent his superior's faith in his abilities as a detective. He resented it even more on his return when he learned that the first in what turned out to be a series of murders had taken place at St Frideswide's Church.

His African tour of duty did, however, spark enough curiosity within Morse to fuel thoughts of an Aegean holiday – certainly enough to talk over the alternative Greek Island cruises with an attractive assistant at the Town and Gown travel agency and take home a full-colour brochure. He even went as far as weighing up the benefits of the drachma exchange rate and buying a Modern Greek phrase-book. But as the weeks passed, the attraction of fourteen days of Mediterranean sunshine seemed inadequate compensation for the flight – the long, long flight as it seemed to him – Morse would be forced to endure to get to Greece.

Morse was not a traveller and nor was he a flyer, character traits ignored by the producers of the television series. In the film version of *The Way Through the Woods*, Morse's superior complains about the summer work overload. 'You've no idea what it was like here,' says Superintendent Strange. 'You only caught the tail end of it…you were off sunning yourself in Beirut.'

'Bayreuth, Sir,' corrects Morse. He was in fact enjoying the annual Wagnerfest in Southern Germany, something he would have loved to do in the novels but never had the nerve.

Another television scenario, proposed by screenwriter Julian Mitchell, has the detective not only agreeing to go to Germany to solve the murder of an opera singer but never returning. Morse is closing on the killer and takes an evening off to attend a performance of Wagner's *Götterdämmerung* in Bayreuth. During the first act a terrorist leaves a bomb in the theatre bar and Morse is killed in the explosion. The idea was abandoned.

Another Julian Mitchell script proposal has Morse crossing the North Sea – once again by plane – to investigate a murder in Holland. To avoid the obvious comparison with *Van der Valk*, Morse was kept well away from Amsterdam and the episode was centred on Dordrecht and Haarlem.

There are times, at least for television consumption, when Morse does enjoy himself abroad. In Italy to investigate fine-art smuggling in *The Death of the Self*, Morse is enchanted by his surroundings while Lewis, desperate to be home to take part in a school fathers' day race, feels isolated and alone.

One day, Mitchell was talking to one of the series' police advisers when the subject of supergrasses came up. John Thaw, the actor who played Morse, was already lobbying for an overseas episode, mainly because it would give the hardworking crew a break and change of surroundings. The result was *Promised Land* in which Morse and Lewis travel to Australia to track down and talk to relocated supergrass Kenny Stone. Once again, the Chief Inspector's fear of flying is conveniently overlooked in favour of exploiting Morse's television alter ego.

Morse much preferred to keep his holidays simple and always travelled by car. It was several weeks after spotting an advertisement in the *Observer* that Morse made the connection with Superintendent Strange's comment on a suitable holiday location – 'Lime, mate! Lime's marvellous!':

"JONGEPI A

THE BAY HOTEL
Lyme Regis

Surely one of the finest settings of any hotel in the West Country! We are the only hotel on the Marine Parade and we enjoy panoramic views from Portland Bill to the east, to the historic Cobb Harbour to the west. The hotel provides a high standard of comfort and cuisine, and a friendly relaxed atmosphere. There are level walks to the shops and harbour, and traffic-free access to the beach, which is immediately in front of the hotel.

For full details please write to

The Bay Hotel, Lyme Regis, Dorset; or just telephone (0297) 442059.

It was another matter persuading his superior to grant him the time off:

> 'I'm not taking more than what's due to me,' protested Morse.
> 'Where are you thinking of?' asked Strange, dunking another chocolate biscuit in his morning tea.
> 'Lyme Regis.'
> 'Ah. Glorious Devon.'
> 'Dorset, sir.'
> 'Next door, surely.'
> '*Persuasion* – it's where some of the scenes in *Persuasion* are set.'
> 'Ah.' Strange looked blank.
> 'And *The French Lieutenant's Woman*,' added Morse.
> 'Ah. I'm with you,' said Strange. 'Saw that at the pictures with the wife...or was it the box?'

Lyme Regis is a two-and-a-half hour drive south from Oxford. The buff-coloured Bay Hotel, with its impressive location only yards from the sea wall, was exactly how Morse had imagined it.

Morse is given Room 27 on the top floor. The room still exists and is regularly requested by dedicated fans retracing the detective's footsteps in *The Way Through the Woods*. As ever, Colin Dexter's description of the seafront hotel is razor sharp – down to the potted palm, billiard table and guinea fowl on the menu.

Historically, Lyme Regis has much the same feel as Oxford. Its mosaic of narrow, winding streets are crammed with summer tourists. Back alleys and cul-de-sacs hide fascinating buildings and still more welcoming pubs and hotels.

The Dutch town of Dordrecht where one abandoned and unfilmed
script would have had Morse investigating a murder

Rising steeply from the sea, the town's origins can be traced back to the eighth century when monks distilled salt water to make various alcoholic drinks. By the thirteenth century, the town had developed into a major British port. Two ships left from Lyme to join the British fleet that confronted the Spanish Armada.

But it was the vast stone Cobb, featured in novels by Jane Austen and John Fowles, that Morse examined from his bedroom window that first morning of his holiday – 'Blast! He'd meant to bring the binoculars.'

Morse intended spending the next seven days on a long-promised 'Coleridge Pilgrimage', touring the West Country in search of the Devon-born poet and philosopher. Although a classics student at Jesus College, Cambridge, it was during an undergraduate walking tour of Oxford that Coleridge was inspired to write some of his earliest poetry.

The next Monday, Morse moved on to the King's Arms in Dorchester and Hardy country. Hardy was the detective's second favourite novelist after Dickens, and *The Mayor of Casterbridge* his second favourite novel after *Bleak House*:

> The building before whose doors [the town band] had pitched their music stands was the chief hotel in Casterbridge – namely, the King's Arms. A spacious bow-window projected into the street over the main portico, and from the open sashes came the babble of voices, the jingle of glasses, and the drawing of corks.
>
> Morse had never enrolled in the itchy-footed regiment of truly adventurous souls, feeling (as he did) little temptation to explore the remoter corners even of his native land; and this, principally, because he could now imagine few if any places closer to his heart than Oxford – the city which, though not his natural mother, had for so many years performed the duties of a loving foster-parent. As for foreign travel, long faded were his boyhood dreams that roamed the sands round Samarkand; and a lifelong pterophobia still precluded any airline bookings to Bayreuth, Salzburg, Vienna – the trio of cities he sometimes thought he ought to see.

'I spent my holiday in cultural pursuits, Lewis, *not* lying on a beach,' snapped Morse in the television episode *Deadly Slumber* when his sergeant offered the image of his boss relaxing on a sun-soaked beach.

In Service of All the Dead *Morse's random attempts at a holiday land him with a rain-soaked week at the Swiss Lodore Hotel, near Keswick*

At other times, Morse looked upon his furloughs from duty with a mixture of guilt and despair. He always felt he should have made better use of his time – 'He was on holiday, and he was going to *have* a holiday' – while desperately hoping something challenging would come up.

In *Service of All the Dead*, his prayers, or at least the prayers of a man who has turned his back on spiritual salvation, are answered, but not before an irrational and haphazard attempt at a holiday. Morse opened the *AA Hotels of Britain* at random and, closing his eyes, stabbed at a left-hand page. It was decided. He would spend the first week of his spring 1979 furlough at the Swiss Lodore Hotel near Keswick.

> On fine days (he had little doubt) the view from his bedroom
> at the Swiss Lodore would have been most beautiful; but the
> mist had driven down from the encircling hills, and it was as
> much as he could do to spot the grass on the lawn below his
> window, with its chairs and tables – all deserted... In his
> bedroom Morse found a leaflet on which was printed Robert
> Southey's *How the Waters Come Down at Lodore*, but he felt
> that even a poet laureate had seldom sunk to such banality.
> And anyway, after three days, Morse knew only too well how
> the waters came down at Lodore – they came down in
> bucketfuls, slanting incessantly in sharp lines from a leaden
> sky.

Back in Oxford, after another stab at the AA guide, Morse drew the line at Inverness. There is, however, one place to which he readily returns. We get a clue in the early pages of *Death is Now My Neighbour*. Morse has completed a cultural questionnaire in the *Police Gazette*. Offered a choice of women to share his final hours on earth, he enthusiastically rejects Princess Diana and Mother Teresa in favour of Kim Basinger. His choice of film was equally suggestive – *Copenhagen Red-Hot Sex*.

Whenever an investigation – *Death is Now My Neighbour*, *The Riddle of the Third Mile* and *Last Seen Wearing* – required a visit to London, Morse would invariably tread the worn and grimy steps of a London strip club.

For Morse 'unbuttoning' was a sexually provocative word
and he never missed a chance to visit the sleazier Soho strip clubs

After The Sexy Susan and The Sensational Sandra even Morse was feeling a little blasé; but, as he explained to an unenthusiastic Lewis, there might be better things to come. And indeed The Voluptuous Vera and The Kinky Kate certainly did something to raise the general standard of the entertainment. There were gimmicks aplenty: fans, whips, bananas and rubber spiders; and Morse dug Lewis in the ribs as an extraordinarily shapely girl, dressed for a fancy-dress ball, titillatingly and tantalisingly divested herself of all but an incongruously ugly mask.

Visiting a strip club gave Morse a sense of precarious adventure. It was the guilt of a voyeur or a peeping Tom or a top-shelf browser. Like one of his favourite poets, Philip Larkin, he got a sexual buzz from the word 'unbuttoning'.

It was magnetic and familiar territory. In the late 1950s when he was a constable stationed at Windsor, he would catch the train from the town's Riverside Station to Waterloo. A short ride on the Northern line to Leicester Square and a leisurely walk up the Charing Cross Road and Morse could lose himself in the warren of Soho back streets.

It was different then. The women walked the streets or clung to street corners in furred and perfumed knots. Someone even produced a booklet – he remembered buying a copy from a news-stand in Wardour Street – full of advertisements paid for by the 'ladies' announcing their individual specialities. Morse also remembered the Old Bailey trial and the publisher's unsuccessful claim that he was providing a public service.

For Morse sexual titillation was quite separate and different from sex. That is not to say that Morse was not a romantic. Acutely aware of his own mental and physical attraction, Morse believed in a certain out-dated protocol in which romance and

While staying at Bath's Royal Crescent Hotel in Death is Now My Neighbour *Morse was finally persuaded to reveal his Christian name*

love and sex are part of a time-honoured progression. He may have found particular women sexually attractive, but he would never have considered bedding them without a degree of good old-fashioned charm and seduction.

Morse's intelligence and self-confidence produce an ageless attraction – especially for nurses. As an undergraduate and not long after his twenty-first birthday, he had invited a 'flighty' little nurse back to his digs in Iffley Road. In *Last Bus to Woodstock*, already past his fiftieth birthday, Morse proved disturbingly appealing to Sue Widdowson, a staff nurse half his age.

There is only one problem – the women to whom Morse is attracted are either too busy, too sensible, or too dangerous. In the television episodes alone, almost half the women he attempts to woo are either implicated in suspicious deaths or the murderers he ultimately arrests.

Thankfully for the reader, not all his relationships are doomed. In *Death is Now My Neighbour*, Morse's stay in hospital is at least made bearable by the attention of Janet McQueen – 'an amply bosomed woman now in her early forties, single and darkly attractive'. With the minutiae of the case left in the capable hands of his sergeant, Morse invites the nursing sister to spend a few days away from Oxford.

> Morse stood for some while on the huge slabs that form the wide pavement stretching along the whole extent of the great 500-foot curve of cinnamon-coloured stone, with its identical façades of double Ionic columns, which comprise Bath's Royal Crescent. It seemed to him a breathtaking architectural masterpiece, with the five-star hotel exactly at its centre: Number 16.

The Royal Crescent Hotel is a Grade I listed building and one of England's finest surviving examples of Georgian architecture. Set in the centre of a grand elliptical curve, its one acre of grounds consists of six elegant and historical buildings.

The Royal Crescent was built to the designs of John Wood the Younger between 1767 and 1774 to meet the individual requirements of wealthy and distinguished visitors to Bath. One early resident was the Duke of York, the second son of George III, who 'engaged the first house in the Royal Crescent' in 1776.

The hotel's opulent atmosphere and a new affair prove a heady and weakening mix for Morse. After twelve novels, and years of speculation in the international press, Colin Dexter decided it was time to share the final mystery of his hero's life. But it was left to Janet McQueen and a romantic weekend in Bath to persuade Morse to reveal a rare display of gratitude – and his Christian name.

On the back of a postcard showing an aerial view of Bath – chosen by his female companion – Morse wrote to Lewis:

> For philistines like you, Lewis, as well as for classical scholars like me, this city with its baths and temples must rank as one of the finest in Europe. You ought to bring the missus here some time.
>
> Did I ever get the chance to thank you for the few (!) contributions you made to our last case together? If I didn't, let me thank you now – let me thank you for everything, my dear old friend.

> Yours aye,
> Endeavour (Morse)

A Morse Compendium

Books

Year	Title	Awards
1975	*Last Bus to Woodstock*	
1977	*Last Seen Wearing*	
1977	*The Silent World of Nicholas Quinn*	
1979	*Service of All the Dead*	*Crime Writers' Association Silver Dagger*
1981	*The Dead of Jericho*	*Crime Writers' Association Silver Dagger*
1983	*The Riddle of the Third Mile*	
1986	*The Secret of Annexe 3*	
1989	*The Wench is Dead*	*Crime Writers' Association Silver Dagger*
1991	*The Jewel That Was Ours*	
1992	*The Way Through the Woods*	*Crime Writers' Association Silver Dagger*
1993	*Morse's Greatest Mystery and Other Stories*	
	Morse's Greatest Mystery	
	Dead as a Dodo	
	Neighbourhood Watch	
	The Inside Story	
	Last Call	
	including five non-Morse stories:	
	Evans Tries an O-Level	
	At the Lulu-Bar Motel	
	A Case of Mis-identity	
	The Carpet-Bagger	
	Monty's Revolver	

1994   *The Daughters of Cain*

1994   *As Good As Gold and Other Stories*

1995   *The Burglar*
        a Morse short story commissioned for the 1995 World Mystery Convention

1995   *Morse's Greatest Mystery and Other Stories*
        new edition including two new short stories
        As Good As Gold
        The Carpet-Bagger

1996   *Death is Now My Neighbour*

1999   *The Remorseful Day*

Omnibus Editions

1991   *First Inspector Morse Omnibus*
        The Dead of Jericho
        Service of All the Dead
        The Silent World of Nicholas Quinn

1991   *Second Inspector Morse Omnibus*
        The Secret of Annexe 3
        The Riddle of the Third Mile
        Last Seen Wearing

1994   *Third Inspector Morse Omnibus*
        Last Bus to Woodstock
        The Wench is Dead
        The Jewel That Was Ours

1998   *Fourth Inspector Morse Omnibus*
        The Way Through the Woods
        The Daughters of Cain
        Death is Now My Neighbour

TV Films

Year	Title	Date broadcast
SERIES ONE		
1987	*The Dead of Jericho*	6 January
1987	*The Silent World of Nicholas Quinn*	13 January
1987	*Service of All the Dead*	20 January
SERIES TWO		
1987	*The Wolvercote Tongue*[1]	25 December
1988	*Last Seen Wearing*	8 March
1988	*The Settling of the Sun*[1]	15 March
1988	*Last Bus to Woodstock*	22 March

SERIES THREE

1989	*Ghost in the Machine*[1]	4 January
1989	*The Last Enemy*[1]	11 January
1989	*Deceived by Flight*[1]	18 January
1989	*The Secret of Bay 5B*[1]	25 January

SERIES FOUR

1990	*The Infernal Serpent*	3 January
1990	*The Sins of the Fathers*	10 January
1990	*Driven to Distraction*	17 January
1990	*Masonic Mysteries*	24 January

SERIES FIVE

1991	*Second Time Around*	20 February
1991	*Fat Chance*	27 February
1991	*Who Killed Harry Field?*	13 March
1991	*Greeks Bearing Gifts*	20 March
1991	*Promised Land*	27 March

SERIES SIX

1992	*Dead on Time*	26 February
1992	*Happy Families*	11 March
1992	*The Death of the Self*	25 March
1992	*Absolute Conviction*	8 April
1992	*Cherubim and Seraphim*	15 April

SERIES SEVEN

1993	*Deadly Slumber*	6 January
1993	*The Day of the Devil*	13 January
1993	*Twilight of the Gods*	20 January

SPECIALS

1995	*The Way Through the Woods*	29 November
1996	*The Daughters of Cain*	27 November
1997	*Death is Now My Neighbour*	19 November
1998	*The Wench is Dead*[2]	11 November
2000	*The Remorseful Day*	15 November

1 Television episodes based on a detailed Colin Dexter story line. *The Wolvercote Tongue* was later developed into the novel *The Jewel That Was Ours*.

2 In the television adaptation, Morse's long-time partner, Sergeant Lewis, is replaced by Detective Constable Adrian Kershaw.

Radio Plays

Title	Broadcast on
Last Bus to Woodstock	BBC Radio 4
The Wench is Dead	BBC Radio 4
Last Seen Wearing[1]	BBC Radio 4
The Silent World of Nicholas Quinn	BBC Radio 4

1 Features an introduction by Colin Dexter.

Music

Year	Title	Label
1991	*Inspector Morse Volume 1*	Virgin
1992	*Inspector Morse Volume 2*	Virgin
1992	*Inspector Morse Volume 3*	Virgin
1995	*The Essential Inspector Morse*	Virgin
1997	*The Passion of Morse*	Tring
2001	*The Magic of Inspector Morse*	Virgin

Fan Club

The Inspector Morse Society, 170 Woodland Road, Sawston, Cambridge, CB2 4DX
(for further information enclose a stamped addressed envelope)

Visitor Information

Information Centres

The Oxford Information Centre
The Old School, Gloucester Green,
Oxford, OX1 2DA
Telephone: (01865) 726871
Fax: (01865) 240261
e-mail: www.oxfordcity.co.uk
Open: Monday–Saturday 09.30–17.00;
Sundays and public holidays 10.00–13.00
and 13.30–15.30 (during summer months)
Closed 25 December–1 January

The Woodstock Visitor Information Centre
Oxfordshire Museum, Park Street,
Woodstock, Oxfordshire, OX20 1SN
Telephone: (01993) 813276

Burford Tourist Information Centre
The Brewery, Sheep Street, Burford,
Oxfordshire, OX18 4LP

Thame Tourist Information Centre
Market House, North Street, Thame,
Oxfordshire, OX9 3HH
Telephone: (01844) 212834

Walking Tours
These leave the Oxford Information
Centre several times per day throughout
the year. A special discount is offered for
groups.
Telephone: (01865) 726871
Inspector Morse Tour: Saturday 13.30 for
2 hours covering between 1 and 2 miles.
Charge: £6.35 adults, £3.50 children (
6–16 years).

Note: there are 19 places on each tour.
Each child must be accompanied by an
adult.

Colleges

Most colleges are open to the public; some
charge a small fee. It is advisable to check
before leaving.

All Souls College
High Street, Oxford, OX1 4AL
Telephone: (01865) 279379
Website: http://www.all-souls.ox.ac.uk
Open: Monday–Friday 14.00–16.00
Charge: none
Note: advance booking is required for
parties of six or more.

Balliol College
Broad Street, Oxford, OX1 3BJ
Telephone: (01865) 277777
Website: http://www.balliol.ox.ac.uk
Open: daily 14.00–17.00
Charge: £1
Note: maximum 10 in a party
at any one time.

Brasenose College
Radcliffe Square, Oxford, OX1 4AJ
Telephone: (01865) 277830
Website: http://www.bnc.ox.ac.uk
Open: daily 10.00–11.30 (tour parties only)
and 14.00–16.30 (17.00 April–October)
Charge: £1 individuals; charges for groups
vary according to the size of the party.

*The impressive Quadrangle at
Brasenose College*

Campion Hall
Brewer Street, Oxford, OX1 1QS
Telephone: (01865) 286100
Not open to visitors.

Christ Church
St Aldate's, Oxford, OX1 1DP
Telephone: (01865) 276150
Website: http://www.chch.ox.ac.uk
Open: every day except Christmas Day,
Monday–Saturday 09.00–17.30; Sunday
12.00–17.30
Charge: £4 adults, £3 concessions,
students and children.
Note: large parties may be split up.
Advance bookings are not required.
Behind-the-scenes tours are available for
an additional fee and must be booked in
advance.

Corpus Christi College
Merton Street, Oxford, OX1 4JF
Telephone: (01865) 276700
Website: http://www.ccc.ox.ac.uk
Open: 13.30–16.30
Charge: none
Note: maximum 20 in a party.

Exeter College
Turl Street, Oxford, OX1 3DP
Telephone: (01865) 279600
Website: http://www.exeter.ox.ac.uk
Open: daily 14.00–17.00
Charge: none
Note: maximum 20 in a party (including
the guide). Advance booking is required.

Green College
Woodstock Road, Oxford, OX2 6HG
Telephone: (01865) 274770
Website: http://www.green.ox.ac.uk

Harris Manchester College
Mansfield Road, Oxford, OX1 3TD
Telephone: (01865) 271006
Website: http://www.hmc.ox.ac.uk
Open: 09.00–12.00; chapel open
08.30–17.30 Monday–Friday
Charge: none

Hertford College
Catte Street, Oxford, OX1 3BW
Telephone: (01865) 279400
Website: http://www.hertford.ox.ac.uk
Open: daily 10.00–12.00 and 14.00 to
dusk
Charge: none
Note: maximum 10 in a group.

Jesus College
Turl Street, Oxford, OX1 3DW
Telephone: (01865) 279700
Website: http://www.jesus.ox.ac.uk
Open: daily 14.00–16.30
Charge: none

Keble College
Parks Road, Oxford, OX1 3PG
Telephone: (01865) 272727
Website: http://www.keble.ox.ac.uk
Open: daily 14.00–17.00
Charge: none

Kellogg College

Wellington Square, Oxford, OX1 2JA
Telephone: (01865) 270383
Website: http://www.kellogg.ox.ac.uk
Open: Monday–Friday 09.00–17.00
Charge: none

Lady Margaret Hall

Norham Gardens, Oxford, OX2 6QA
Telephone: (01865) 274300
Website: http://www.lmh.ox.ac.uk
Open: 10.00–17.00
Charge: none

Linacre College

St Cross Road, Oxford, OX1 3JA
Telephone: (01865) 271650
Website: http://www.linacre.ox.ac.uk
Open: check with the Porter's Lodge
Charge: none

Lincoln College

Turl Street, Oxford, OX1 3DR
Telephone: (01865) 279800
Website: http://www.linc.ox.ac.uk
Open: Monday–Friday 14.00–17.00;
Sunday 11.00–17.00
Charge: none (groups are invited to
make a donation)

Magdalen College

High Street, Oxford, OX1 4AU
Telephone: (01865) 276000
Website: http://www.magd.ox.ac.uk
Open: 14.00–18.00, or dusk if earlier, 1
October–20 June; 12.00–18.00 25 June–
30 September
Charge: £2 adults, £1 concessions,
children, pre-booked groups (13
April–30 September). Residents of
Oxford are not charged at any time.
Note: maximum 20 people in a group.

Mansfield College

Mansfield Road, Oxford, OX1 3TF
Telephone: (01865) 270999
Website: http://www.mansfield.ox.ac.uk
Open: 09.00–17.00 by prior request
Charge: none
Note: quad and chapel only.

Merton College

Merton Street, Oxford, OX1 4JD
Telephone: (01865) 276310
Website: http://www.merton.ox.ac.uk
Open: Monday–Friday 14.00–16.00;
Saturday–Sunday 10.00–16.00
Charge: none for college grounds. Tours
of the Old Library may be available at £1
per person.
Note: parties of 10 or more must be
accompanied by a Blue Badge Guide and
book in advance.

New College

New College Lane, Oxford, OX1 3BN
Telephone: (01865) 279555
Website: http://www.new.ox.ac.uk
Open: 11.00–17.00 Easter–October (via
New College Lane Gate); 14.00–16.00
October–Easter (via Holywell Street
Gate)
Charge: £2 adults, £1 children, unwaged,
Easter–October; no charge at other
times. Residents of Oxford are not
charged at any time.
Note: maximum 10 in a group.

Nuffield College
New Road, Oxford, OX1 1NF
Telephone: (01865) 278500
Website: http://www.nuff.ox.ac.uk
Open: 09.00–17.00
Charge: none
Note: maximum 6 people at one time.

Oriel College
Oriel Square, Oxford, OX1 4EW
Telephone: (01865) 276555
Website: http://www.oriel.ox.ac.uk
Open: daily 14.00–17.00
Charge: none
Note: parties of 20 or more must book in advance.

Pembroke College
St Aldate's, Oxford, OX1 1DW
Telephone: (01865) 276444
Website: http://www.pmb.ox.ac.uk
Open: by prior appointment only
Charge: none
Note: maximum 20 people in a group. Must be accompanied by an official guide.

The Queen's College
High Street, Oxford, OX1 4AW
Telephone: (01865) 279120
Website: http://www.queens.ox.ac.uk
Open: by prior appointment only
Charge: none
Note: groups only. Must be accompanied by an official guide.

Regent's Park College
Pusey Street, Oxford, OX1 2LB
Telephone: (01865) 288120
Not open to the public.

St Anne's College
Woodstock Road, Oxford, OX2 6HS
Telephone: (01865) 274800
Website: http://www.stannes.ox.ac.uk
Open: Monday–Saturday 09.30–16.00;
Sunday 12.00–16.00
Charge: none

St Antony's College
Woodstock Road, Oxford, OX2 6JF
Telephone: (01865) 284700
Website: http://www.sant.ox.ac.uk

St Benet's Hall
38 St Giles', Oxford, OX1 3LN
Telephone: (01865) 280054
Not open to the public.

St Catherine's College
Manor Road, Oxford, OX1 3UJ
Telephone: (01865) 271700
Website: http://www.stcatz.ox.ac.uk
Open: 09.00–17.00
Charge: none

St Cross College
St Giles', Oxford, OX1 3LZ
Telephone: (01865) 278490
Website: http://www.stx.ox.ac.uk

St Edmund Hall
Queen's Lane, Oxford, OX1 4AR
Telephone: (01865) 279000
Website: http://www.seh.ox.ac.uk
Open: daylight hours
Charge: none
Note: maximum 12 people in a group.
Must report to the Lodge upon arrival.

St Hilda's College
Cowley Place, Oxford, OX4 1DY
Telephone: (01865) 276884
Website: http://www.sthildas.ox.ac.uk
Open: Monday–Friday 14.00–17.00
Charge: none
Note: parties must book in advance.

St Hugh's College
St Margaret's Road, Oxford, OX2 6LE
Telephone: (01865) 274900
Website: http://www.st-hughs.ox.ac.uk
Open: daily 10.00–16.00
Charge: none
Note: groups of 6 or more must book in
advance.

St John's College
St Giles', Oxford, OX1 3JP
Telephone: (01865) 277300
Website: http://www.sjc.ox.ac.uk
Open: 13.00–17.00 (or dusk if earlier)
Charge: none
Note: maximum 15 in a group; larger
groups will be split. Must be
accompanied by a guide.

St Peter's College
New Inn Hall Street, Oxford, OX1 2DL
Telephone: (01865) 278900
Website: http://www.spc.ox.ac.uk
Open: 10.00 to dusk
Charge: none
Note: groups of 5 or more must book in
advance.

Somerville College
Woodstock Road, Oxford, OX2 6HD
Telephone: (01865) 270600
Website: http://www.some.ox.ac.uk
Open: 14.00–17.30. Mornings for groups
accompanied by a guide
Charge: none
Note: maximum 20 in a group.

Templeton College
Kennington Road, Oxford, OX1 5NY
Telephone: (01865) 422500
Website: http://www.templeton.ox.ac.uk

Trinity College
Broad Street, Oxford, OX1 3BH
Telephone: (01865) 279900
Website: http://www.trinity.ox.ac.uk
Open: 10.00–12.00 and 14.00–16.00
Charge: £2 adults, £1 seniors, children
(summer); £1 adults, 50p concesions,
children (winter).
Note: maximum 25 in a group
accompanied by a guide.

University College
High Street, Oxford, OX1 4BH
Telephone: (01865) 276602
Website: http://www.univ.ox.ac.uk

Wadham College is the youngest of the University's 'old' foundations

Wadham College
Parks Road, Oxford, OX1 3PN
Telephone: (01865) 277900
Website: http://www.wadham.ox.ac.uk
Open: 13.00–16.15 term time;
10.30–11.45 and 13.00–16.15 during
vacations
Charge: none
Note: groups must book in advance and
be accompanied by a guide.

Wolfson College
Linton Road, Oxford, OX2 6UD
Telephone: (01865) 274100
Website: http://www.wolfson.ox.ac.uk
Open: gardens open in daylight hours
Charge: none
Note: groups should notify the Lodge in
advance.

Worcester College
Walton Street, Oxford, OX1 2HB
Telephone: (01865) 278300
Website: http://www.worcester.ox.ac.uk
Open: daily 14.00–17.00
Charge: none
Note: maximum 8 in a group. Tour
groups must book in advance.

Museums

Ashmolean Museum
Beaumont Street, Oxford, OX1 2PH
Telephone: (01865) 278000
Open: Tuesday–Saturday 10.00–16.00;
Sundays 14.00–16.00; bank holiday
Mondays 14.00–16.00
Charge: none (voluntary donations)
Note: features British and European
paintings from the Middle Ages to the
present day. Also on show: classical and
oriental art, including Chinese bronzes,
Islamic and Japanese ceramics and
Indian sculpture, as well as silver, glass
and porcelain.

Bate Collection
Faculty of Music, St Aldate's, Oxford,
OX1 1DB
Telephone: (01865) 276139
Open: Monday–Friday 14.00–17.00;
Saturday 10.00–12.00 (during full term
only)
Charge: none

Museum of the History of Science
Old Ashmolean Building, Broad Street,
Oxford, OX1 3AZ
Telephone: (01865) 277280
Open: Tuesday–Saturday 12.00–16.00
Closed bank holidays and Christmas
week.
Charge: none

Museum of Modern Art

30 Pembroke Street, Oxford, OX1 1BP
Telephone: (01865) 722733
Open: Tuesday–Sunday 11.00–18.00;
Thursday 11.00–19.00
Charge: £2.50 adults, £1.50 concessions,
under 16s free.

Museum of Oxford

Town Hall, St Aldate's, Oxford, OX1
1DZ
Telephone: (01865) 252761
Open: Tuesday–Friday 10.00–16.00;
Saturday10.00–17.00; Sunday
12.00–16.00
Charge: £2.00 adults, £1.50 concessions
and 50p children.

Oxford University of Museum of Natural History

Parks Road, Oxford, OX1 3PW
Telephone: (01865) 270949
Open: Monday–Sunday 12.00–17.00
Charge: none

Pitt-Rivers Museum – Anthropology and Archaeology

Parks Road, Oxford, OX1 3PP
Telephone: (01865) 270927
Open: Monday–Saturday 13.00–16.30;
Sunday 14.00–16.30
Charge: none
Note: entrance via University Museum.

Oxford University Press Museum

Great Clarendon Street, Oxford, OX2
6DP
Telephone: (01865) 267572
Open: normal office hours
Charge: none

The Oxfordshire Museum

Fletcher's House, Park Street,
Woodstock, OX20 1SN
Telephone: (01993) 811456
Open: Tuesday–Saturday 10.00–17.00;
Sunday 14.00–17.00
Charge: £1 adults, 50p concessions,
children free.
Note: galleries include Roman
Oxfordshire, the Woodstock Gallery, the
Picture Gallery, the Children's Gallery,
the Treasure's Gallery, the Innovations
Gallery and Landscape Galleries.

Oxford Museums Store

Witney Road, Standlake, Oxford, OX8
7QG
Telephone: (01865) 300972
Open: by appointment
Charge: none

The Oxford Story

6 Broad Street, Oxford, OX1 3AJ
Telephone: (01865) 790055
Note: exhibition interpreting the 800-
year history of Oxford University.
Charge: £6.50 adults, £5.50 concessions
and £5.00 children.

Oxford Bus Museum
British Rail Yard, Long Hanborough,
OX8 8LA
Telephone: (01993) 883617
Open: Sunday 10.30–16.30
Charge: £3 adults, £1.50 concessions and
children.
Note: a collection of mainly City of
Oxford Motor Services vehicles, dating
from 1915 to the 1960s.

Tolsey Museum
High Street, Burford, OX18 4QU
Telephone: (01367) 810294
Open: 14.00–17.00 (weekends and bank
holidays 11–17.00) March–November
Charge: 72p adults, 50p concessions,
children free.

Galleries

Balfour Galleries
Pitt-Rivers Museum Annexe, Banbury
Road, Oxford, OX2 6PN
Telephone: (01865) 270927
Open: Saturday 13.00–16.30; weekdays
by appointment only.

Christ Church Picture Gallery
Christ Church, Canterbury Gate, Oriel
Square, Oxford, OX1 1DP
Telephone: (01865) 276172
Open: Monday–Saturday 10.30–13.00
and 14.00–17.30; Sunday 14.00–17.30;
closes 16.30 October–Easter

Charge: £1 adults, 50p concessions.
Note: features 14th–18th century art.

Oxford Gallery
23 High Street, Oxford, OX1 4AH
Telephone: (01865) 242731
Open: Monday–Saturday 10.00–17.00
Charge: none
Note: high-quality exhibitions and good
selection of prints, jewellery, ceramics,
glass, wood and textiles.

Library

Bodleian Library
Broad Street, Oxford, OX1 3BG
Telephone: (01865) 277188
Open: Monday–Friday 09.00–17.00;
Saturday 09.00–12.30
Charge: £3.50
Note: one-hour guided tours.

Wild Life Park

Cotswold Wildlife Park
Burford, Oxfordshire, OX18 4JW
Telephone: (01993) 823006
Open: daily 10.00–17.00
March–September; 10.00–16.00 October;
10.00–15.30 November–February
Closed Christmas Day
Charge: £6.50 adults, £4.00 concessions
and children; under 3s free.

Stately Home

Blenheim Palace
Evesham Road, Woodstock, OX20 1PX
Telephone: (01993) 811325
Open: The Palace: daily 10.30–17.30
11 March–31 October. The Park: daily
09.00–17.00. The Pleasure Gardens,
Marlborough Maze and Butterfly House:
10.00–18.00 mid-March–October
Charge: £10 adults, £7.50 concessions and
16- and 17-year-olds, £5 children 5–15.
Note: admission to the Palace includes a
tour, Sir Winston Churchill exhibition,
park, gardens, parking, butterfly house
and train. Entry to the Marlborough
Maze is extra. Maximum 30 people in a
group.

Churches

City Church of St Michael-at-the-North Gate
Cornmarket Street, Oxford
Telephone: (01865) 240940
Open: daily 10.00–17.00 April–October;
10.00–16.00 November–March;
12.00–17.00 Sundays. Closed during
services and Christmas Day
Charge (tower): £1.50 adults, £1
concessions, 80p children.

University Church of St Mary the Virgin
High Street, Oxford, OX1 3TA
Telephone: (01865) 243806
Open: Monday–Saturday 09.15–16.30
(high summer 18.30); Sundays
12.30–17.00

Carfax Tower
Carfax, Oxford
Telephone: (01865) 792653
Open: 10.00–17.30 April–October;
10.00–15.30 November–March (closed
Christmas week)
Charge: £1.20 adults, 60p children.

Theatres

The Apollo Theatre
George Street, Oxford, OX1 2AG
Box-office telephone: 0870 6063500
Charge: £3.50–£7.50 for regular events;
£6–£20 for top star entertainment.

The Burton-Taylor Theatre
Gloucester Street, Oxford, OX1 2BN
Box-office telephone: (01865) 305305

Holywell Music Room
Holywell Street, Oxford, OX1 2BN
Box-office telephone: (01865) 798600
Note: the oldest music room in Europe.

The Newman Rooms
Rose Place, St Aldate's, Oxford
Telephone: (01865) 722651
Charge: from £2.50

Oxford Playhouse
11–12 Beaumont Street, Oxford, OX4
1RE
Box-office telephone: (01865) 798600

The Old Fire Station
40 George Street, Oxford
Telephone: (01865) 297170
Note: features a studio theatre and art
gallery, a hands-on science exhibition
and a café-bar with live music

Pegasus Theatre
Magdalen Road, off Iffley Road, Oxford,
OX4 1RE
Box-office telephone: (01865) 722851
Open: Saturdays; youth theatre activities
Tuesday 20.00

Sheldonian Theatre
Broad Street, Oxford, OX1 3AZ
Telephone: (01865) 277299
Open: Monday–Saturday 10.00–12.30
and 14.00–16.30 (15.30 in winter)
Charge: £1.50 adults, £1 children under 15.

Note: opening hours are curtailed when
the theatre is in use for university
ceremonies, meetings or concerts.

Gardens

Christ Church Meadow
St Aldate's, Oxford
Open: daily 07.00–21.00
Charge: none

Note: herbaceous-bordered memorial
garden, river walks and squirrels.
Nearest green space to city centre.

Port Meadow
entrance via Walton Well Road, Thames
Towpath or Wolvercote village
Open: common land
Charge: none

Note: largest green space in Oxford.
Location for the Oxford Horse Races.
First-class cricket ground open
08.00–21.00, no charge (donation).

University of Oxford Botanic Garden
Rose Lane, Oxford, OX1 4AX
Telephone: (01865) 286690
Open: 09.00–17.00 (16.30 in winter),
glasshouses 14.00–16.30. Closed
Christmas Day and Good Friday.
Charge: £2 April–August (free at other
times).
Note: last admission 16.15

University Parks
Parks office, South Parks Road, Oxford,
OX1 3RF
Telephone: (01865) 282400
Open: all gates are open by 07.45.
Closing times vary according to the time
of year.
Charge: none

Other sites of interest

Castle
Between New Road and Paradise Street,
Oxford
Open: tours can be arranged through the
Museum of Oxford.
Charge: £2 adults, £1 children.

City Walls
Note: the walls are still visible and give
an idea of the size of medieval Oxford.
The City Church of St Michael-at-the-
North Gate in Cornmarket Street, the
Eastgate Hotel in High Street, and the
Westgate Shopping Centre at the west
end of Queen Street mark the sites of the
three main entrances to the city. The best
stretch is in New College.

Combe Mill
near Long Hanborough, Woodstock
Telephone: (01865) 880356
Open: 17 May, 16 August and 18 October
Charge: £2 adults, £1 concessions and
children.
Note: working steam engine and
waterwheel. Blacksmith at work and
local church tower clocks.

Harcourt Arboretum
Nuneham Courtney, Oxfordshire
Telephone: (01865) 343501
Open: daily 10.00–17.00 May–October;
Monday–Friday 10.00–16.30
November–April

Oxon & Bucks Light Infantry
TA Centre, Slade Park, Oxford, OX3 7JJ
Telephone: (01865) 780128

Picture credits

Index

Alfred the Great 90–1
Amis, Kingsley 30
Anglo-Catholic Oxford Movement 99
Archer, Jeffrey 35
architecture, Oxford University 40
Arnold, Matthew 36–7, 61, 128–9
Ashmole, Elias 93
Ashmolean Museum 90–1, 93
Auden, W.H. 40
Austen, Jane 180

Balliol College 38, 42, 43
Bath 186–7
Bear Inn, Oxford 56–8
Beaufort College (fictional) 38
Beaumont College 26
Bedwell, Brian 150
Benn, Tony 40
Betjeman, Sir John 124, 129, 167
Black Death 40
Black Prince Pub, Woodstock 50
Blackwell's bookshop 122–7
Blake, Nicholas (Cecil Day Lewis) 111
Blenheim Palace 153–8, 160
Boat Inn, Thrupp 66–7
Bodleian Library, Oxford 118–22
Bodley, Thomas 38, 121, 122
Bookbinders Arms, Canal Street 85

books, Morse's choice of 127
Brasenose College 33, 35
Bream, Sir Clixby (Master of Lonsdale) 26,
    36, 37
breweries, in Oxford 48–9
Broad Street 25
Browne-Smith, Dr (Morse's classics tutor)
    29, 31
Buchan, John 35
Burford 160–1
Burghley House 167
Burton, Robert 35

Canning, George 40
Cardinal College *see* Christ Church College
Carr, John Dickson 108
Carroll, Lewis (Charles Dodgson) 40, 61, 128
Cecil, William 167
Chaucer, Geoffrey 38, 157
Cherubim and Seraphim 163
Christ Church College 26, 40
Churchill, John, 1st Duke of Marlborough
    153, 157–8
Churchill, Lord Randolph 38
Churchill, Sir Winston 160
Civil War 63, 167
Coghill, Neville 129
'Coleridge Pilgrimage' 180

Cook, Captain James 165, 174
Courtenay College 26
Cranmer, Thomas, Archbishop of
        Canterbury 99
crime writers 108–17
Crispin, Edmund (Robert Bruce
        Montgomery) 108–11
crosswords, Morse's compulsion for 115, 117

Dalgliesh, Adam 114
Day Lewis, Cecil 111
de Bryn, Max (pathologist) 100, 144, 147
Dead on Time 26, 43
Deadly Slumber 180
Death is Now My Neighbour 26, 31, 36, 50,
        56, 67, 74, 117, 140, 183, 186
death
    Morse's views on 48
    of Morse 134
Defoe, Daniel 18, 121–2
'Desert Island Discs', Morse's selection 45
Dexter, Colin 114–17
Dickens, Charles 180
Dodgson, Charles (Lewis Carroll) 40, 61, 128
dons 26, 40, 45

Eagle and Child public house 129
Eden, Anthony 40
Edward the Elder, King of Wessex 16–17
Eliot, T.S. 38
Exeter College 43

Fat Chance 26, 40
Fen, Gervase 110–11
Fiennes, Celia 167
Fowles, John 40, 180
Friar Bacon Pub, Elsfield (now demolished)
        59

Galsworthy, John 40
Ghost in the Machine 26
Gladstone, William 40
Godstow Nunnery 61–2

Golding, William 35
Grahame, Kenneth 100
Graves, Robert 30
Great Western Railway 19, 22
Green College 43

Haig, Earl, Field Marshall 35
Hardy, Thomas 85, 176, 180
Haworth Hotel, Oxford 50
Hawthorne, Nathaniel 73
health, Morse's problems with 73–4
Henry I 17
Henry II 62
Henry VIII 40, 62–3
Holmes, Sherlock 111–12
Holywell Cemetery 100
Hoskins, W.G. 167
Housman, A.E. 30, 45, 176
Huxley, Professor Thomas 89

Inklings literary group 129

James, P.D. 114
Jericho area 80, 82, 84–5
Jericho Tavern 82, 85
John Radcliffe Hospital 23
Jude the Obscure 85

Keble College 43
Kemp, Theodore 36, 100
Kidlington 135, 136
Kristofferson, Kris 38

Lady Margaret Hall 42
Larkin, Philip 30, 108, 185
Last Bus to Woodstock 31, 50, 73, 108, 114–15,
        117, 136, 139, 140, 141, 153, 157, 186
Last Call 67
Last Seen Wearing 40, 49, 127, 140, 144, 183
Latimer, Hugh, Bishop of Worcester 99
Lawrence, T.E. 117–18
Lewis, C.S. 43, 129

Lewis, Sergeant Robert 50, 54–5, 67, 117–18,
    129, 140–1, 143–4
Lewis, Valerie (wife of Sergeant Lewis) 144
Linacre College 43
Liverpool, Lord 40
locations 147–161
Lonsdale College (fictional) 26, 31, 33
Lyme Regis 177, 179–10

Macmillan, Frederick 122–4
Magdalen Bridge 19
Magdalen College 26, 43
Martyrs Memorial 99
Masonic Mysteries 136
McQueen, Janet 186–7
Merton College 26, 38, 55
Mitre Inn, Oxford (now a restaurant) 58–9
Montgomery, Robert Bruce 108–11
Morris, Willam, Lord Nuffield 23
Morse (personal information)
    in Africa 97, 176
    and alcohol 47–50
    in Australia 177
    age of 136, 139
    and books 127
    Christian name 165, 186–7
    and Clare Osborne 31
    compulsion for crosswords 115, 117
    death of 134
    views on death 48
    'Desert Island Discs' 45
    dislike of travel 164, 176–7
    early life 163, 164–5, 168–76
    in Germany 177
    health problems 73–4
    and holidays 176–7, 179–80, 183
    in Italy 177
    and Janet McQueen 186–7
    London strip clubs 183,185
    on marriage 164
    and money 54
    national service 174, 176
    passion for poetry 127–9

    phobias 66
    in the police force 134–6, 139
    relationship with parents 164, 165, 172,
        173–4
    on religion and life 94
    resistance to change 163, 164
    and romance 185–6
    at St John's College 26–30
    and Wendy Spencer 29, 30, 43, 71
    and women 164
    working methods 139–40
Morse's Greatest Mystery 54
Mortimer, John 35
Murder on the Oxford Canal 63, 75, 118
Museum of Oxford 94

Neighbourhood Watch 45
New Bodleian Library, Oxford 118–21
New College 26, 38–40
North Oxford (location of Morse's flat) 45,
    60
Nuffield College 43

Old Parsonage Hotel, North Oxford 50,
    53–4
Osborne, Clare 31
Oxford
    breweries 48–9
    Carfax tower 17
    dons 26, 40, 45
    early history 15–23
    Morse's association with 107–8
    St Frideswide, patron saint 16, 97
    tourism 23
    Town Hall 94
Oxford Canal 80, 82, 84
Oxford Canal murder 75, 77, 80
Oxford disease 36–7
Oxford Gazette (later the London Gazette)
    107
Oxford University 25–45, 37–8 (*see also*
    individual colleges)
    architecture 40

Oxford University Press 23

Palin, Michael 35
Parson's Pleasure 104
Peel, Sir Robert 40
Penn, William 40
Pevsner, Sir Nikolaus 167
phobias, which Morse suffered 66
Pitt-Rivers Museum 89–90
Plough Inn, Wolvercote Green 63
poetry, Morse's passion for 127–9
police force, Morse's career 134–6, 139
Pope, Alexander 158
Promised Land 177

Queens College 40

Radcliffe, Dr John 35
Radford's brewery 48–9
Randolph Hotel, Oxford 67–8, 71
Ridley, Nicholas, Bishop of London 99
Rosamund the Fair 62
Royal Crescent Hotel, Bath 186–7

Saxons 15–16
Sayers, Dorothy L. 112–14
Scarman, Lord 35
Scott, Sir Walter 167
scouts 26
Second Time Around 71
Second World War 168, 169
Selwood, Edward 53–4
Service of All the Dead 55, 71, 176, 97, 100,
    117, 136, 164, 183
Shadowlands 43
Shaw, George Bernard 37
Smith, Adam 37
Somerville College 42–3
SPARTA 49
Spencer, Wendy 29, 30, 43, 71
St Anne's College 44
St Anthony's College 43
St Barnabas' Church, Jericho 85

St Bernard's College 30
St Birinus 16
St Catherine's College 44
St Cross Church, Holywell 100
St Frideswide, patron saint of Oxford 16, 97
St Giles' 30, 53, 68
St Hilda's College 43
St Hugh's College 43
St John's College 26–30, 53, 108
St Mary Magdalen Church 97
St Mary the Virgin Church 98–9
St Michael-by-the-North-Gate Church 97
St Peter's College 44
St Saviour's College 26
St Scholastica's Day riot (1355) 38, 98
Stainer, Sir John 100
Stamford, Lincolnshire (Morse's birthplace)
    30, 33, 164, 165–73
Stamford Grammar School 172–3
Strange, Superintendant 163, 177, 179
Strangeways, Nigel 111
Swindlestock Tavern, St Aldate's 98

television, adaptation for 131, 134, 136,
    147–61
Thames Valley Police 135–6
The Anatomy of Melancholy 35
The Carpet Bagger 176
The Daughter of Time 77
The Daughters of Cain 26, 36, 40, 47, 54, 55,
    73, 85, 89, 105, 139
The Dead of Jericho 26, 33, 43, 80, 82, 85, 127,
    131–2, 139, 140
The Death of the Self 177
The Infernal Serpent 26, 38
The Jewel That Was Ours 36, 61, 71, 90, 93,
    94, 99, 100, 139
The Last Enemy 26, 36, 67, 73, 107
The Lord of the Rings 129
The Remorseful Day 60, 67, 71, 134, 139, 160
The Riddle of the Third Mile 30, 31, 33, 67, 73,
    183
The Secret of Annexe 3 43, 50, 53, 58, 60

The Secret of Bay 5B 40

The Settling of the Sun 26, 37, 176

The Silent World of Nicholas Quinn 40–2, 48,
      55, 74, 160

The Sins of the Fathers 48

The Way Through the Woods 31, 61, 66, 147,
      150, 153, 157, 177, 179

The Wench is Dead 73, 74, 75–7, 118

The Wolvercote Tongue 71, 90, 93, 139

The World of Inspector Morse 176

ties, at the Bear Inn, Oxford 56–8

Tolkien, J.R.R. 129

tourism, in Oxford 23

Town Hall, Oxford 94

Tradescant, John 93

Trinity College 49

Trout Inn, Lower Wolvercote 61–3, 128

Turf Tavern, Oxford 55

Twilight of the Gods 26, 43, 122

Tynan, Ken 100

University College 26, 38

University Museum 89

University Parks 104

Vanbrugh, Sir John 158

Wagner 45, 176

Walpole, Horace 158

Waugh, Auberon 40

Wealth of Nations 37

Wedgewood, Lady 167

White, Sir Thomas 30

White Hart, Wytham 66

Who Killed Harry Field? 26

Wilberforce, Samuel, Bishop of Oxford 89

Wilde, Oscar 43, 53

Williams, Charles 129

Wimsey, Lord Peter 114

Wolfson College 43

Wolsey College 26

Wolvercote village 61

women's colleges 42–3

Woodstock 153, 157

Woodstock Arms, Oxford 60

Wytham Woods 147, 150, 153